TABLE OF CONTENTS

Foreword

In the age of accelerating technological advancements, we find ourselves standing at the precipice of an extraordinary era. The realm of Artificial Intelligence (AI) is no longer confined to the pages of science fiction but has firmly rooted itself in the fabric of our reality. It is a time when the lines between the capabilities of machines and the essence of humanity blur, where the convergence of technology and human aspiration propels us toward a future both remarkable and uncertain.

"Redefining Tomorrow: Exploring the Boundaries of AI and Humanity" by AI Mad Scientist invites you to embark on a journey into this thrilling and transformative epoch. Within these pages, you will find a roadmap that transcends conventional boundaries and challenges preconceived notions about our relationship with AI. This book is a testament to the human spirit's capacity to adapt, evolve, and thrive in an ever-changing world.

The author, AI Mad Scientist has sought to delve deep into the heart of our AI-infused world, exploring its implications, ethics, and limitless potential. But beyond the technical marvels, this book is a celebration of what it means to be human. It's about our curiosity, our resilience, and our ability to shape the future, even in the face of daunting technological change.

Through interviews with experts, anecdotes from everyday life, and a journey through the latest AI breakthroughs, "Redefining Tomorrow" examines how AI is reshaping our industries, economies, and even our personal lives. It navigates the ethical and philosophical questions that arise as machines become more intelligent and intertwined with our existence.

Yet, this book is not solely about the machines themselves; it's about us, the creators and cohabitants of this new world. It's about the opportunities we have to harness AI as a tool for progress, to augment our capabilities, and to solve some of the most pressing challenges facing humanity.

So, whether you are a technophile eager to understand the intricacies of AI or a curious soul looking for insights into our collective future, I invite you to open these pages with an open mind and a sense of wonder. "Redefining Tomorrow" is not just a book; it's a conversation, a call to action, and an exploration of the human spirit in the age of AI.

As we embark on this journey together, let us remember that our future is not predetermined by machines but shaped by the choices we make today. Let us embrace the potential of AI with optimism, responsibility, and a commitment to a brighter tomorrow.

Welcome to "Redefining Tomorrow."

AI Mad Scientist
[September, 2023]

Acknowledgments

Writing a book is a journey that doesn't happen in isolation. It's a culmination of countless hours of research, reflection, and collaboration with individuals whose support and contributions have been invaluable.

I would like to express my deep gratitude to the following individuals and groups:

AI Thought Leaders and Innovators: I extend my heartfelt thanks to the AI researchers, scientists, and innovators who generously shared their knowledge and insights. Your passion for pushing the boundaries of AI and your dedication to advancing our understanding of this field has been instrumental in shaping this book.

My Family: To my family, whose unwavering support and encouragement sustained me throughout this endeavor, I am profoundly grateful. Your belief in the importance of this work has been my driving force.

My Editor and Publishing Team: To my editor and the entire publishing team, thank you for your guidance, expertise, and commitment to bringing this book to fruition. Your contributions have transformed my ideas into a coherent and engaging narrative.

Peer Reviewers and Beta Readers: I extend my appreciation to the peer reviewers and beta readers who provided valuable feedback and helped refine the content of this book. Your insights improved the quality and clarity of the material.

Mentors and Colleagues: I am fortunate to have had the guidance and mentorship of esteemed colleagues who have shaped my perspective on AI and its implications. Your mentorship has been instrumental in my growth as an author and thinker.

Readers and Supporters: To the readers and supporters of my work, thank you for your curiosity, engagement, and enthusiasm. Your interest in the subject matter motivates me to continue exploring the frontiers of AI and humanity.

The OpenAI Team: I owe a debt of gratitude to the dedicated team at OpenAI, whose pioneering work in AI research has expanded the boundaries of human knowledge. Your contributions to the field have inspired many, including myself.

The Future: Finally, to the future itself, where AI continues to evolve and shape our world, I dedicate this book. May we approach the challenges and opportunities it presents with wisdom, compassion, and a commitment to the betterment of humanity?

This book is a testament to the collaborative spirit that drives progress in the age of AI. While my name may appear on the cover, it represents the collective effort of a diverse and passionate community. Thank you for being a part of this remarkable journey.

AI Mad Scientist

Introduction

In the vast tapestry of human history, there are moments when the very fabric of our existence seems to shimmer with anticipation. It's as if the universe itself holds its breath, awaiting the culmination of centuries of innovation, imagination, and ambition. We are living in one such moment—the age of artificial intelligence.

The story of AI is a story of human ingenuity, a narrative that spans millennia, from the myths of ancient gods breathing life into inanimate statues to the sophisticated algorithms that now power our digital lives. It is a tale of relentless pursuit—the pursuit of intelligence, of understanding, and, ultimately, of transcendence.

In the pages that follow, we embark on a journey into the heart of this extraordinary era. It is a journey that delves into the origins of AI, from the dreams of ancient mythologies to the Turing machines of the 20th century. It takes us through the annals of science fiction, where visionaries dared to imagine machines that could think and feel, and it brings us face to face with the ethical dilemmas that arise as AI becomes woven into the fabric of our daily lives.

But this journey is not just a retrospective—it's a forward-looking exploration of the potential and the promise of artificial intelligence. It's a quest to understand how AI is transforming industries, amplifying human potential, and redefining the very essence of what it means to be human. It's an inquiry into the ethical considerations that demand our attention as AI becomes an integral part of our society.

The age of AI is not a distant future; it's our present reality. It's the voice-activated assistant that responds to our queries, the recommendation algorithm that suggests our next read, and the autonomous vehicle that navigates our streets. It's the technology that powers medical diagnoses, predicts financial trends, and fosters creativity in unexpected ways.

As we navigate this age of AI, we must be both explorers and stewards, boldly venturing into uncharted territory while ensuring that the path we blaze is one of ethical responsibility and human flourishing. The challenges are immense, but so are the possibilities.

This book is an invitation to join me on this journey—a journey into the heart of AI and its profound impact on our human future. It's a journey that will take us from the birth of AI to its current state, from its pioneers to its ethical dilemmas, and from its augmentation of human intelligence to the uncharted territory of tomorrow.

As we embark on this exploration, let us remember that the story of AI is not just about machines; it's about us—the dreamers, the innovators, and the stewards of our shared destiny. It's about redefining tomorrow in the age of AI.

Part I: The Age of AI Unveiled

In this chapter, we unveil the transformative impact of artificial intelligence (AI) in our modern world. The Age of AI represents a paradigm shift, characterized by unprecedented technological advancements, societal changes, and ethical considerations.

At the heart of the Age of AI lies data—the lifeblood of AI systems. The exponential growth of data, fueled by the digitalization of our lives, serves as the raw material for AI algorithms. Big data analytics, coupled with AI, enables us to extract insights, patterns, and predictions from vast datasets, revolutionizing industries such as healthcare, finance, and marketing.

In the Age of AI, healthcare has undergone a remarkable transformation. AI-powered diagnostic tools enhance the accuracy and speed of disease detection. Machine learning models predict patient outcomes, enabling personalized treatment plans. Robotic surgery systems, guided by AI, assist surgeons in complex procedures. The fusion of AI and healthcare improves patient care, reduces medical errors, and extends our understanding of diseases.

The financial industry embraces AI to manage risk, detect fraud, and optimize investments. Algorithmic trading powered by AI outpaces human traders. AI-driven chatbots provide customer support and streamline operations. The Age of AI introduces FinTech innovations, from robo-advisors to blockchain applications, reshaping the financial landscape.

Transportation experiences a revolution as AI takes the wheel. Self-driving cars navigate streets, promising safer and more efficient transportation. AI algorithms optimize traffic flow, reducing congestion and emissions. Drones equipped with AI perform tasks from package delivery to search and rescue. The Age of AI in transportation ushers in a new era of mobility.

AI's impact extends to education and research. Intelligent tutoring systems adapt to students' learning styles, improving educational outcomes. Researchers leverage AI to analyze massive datasets, accelerating scientific discoveries. The Age of AI enhances the accessibility of education and the pace of innovation.

As AI's influence grows, ethical dilemmas come to the forefront. Questions about bias and fairness in AI algorithms arise. Concerns regarding data privacy and surveillance challenge the boundaries of technology and personal rights. Ethical AI research and responsible development become critical considerations in the Age of AI.

The Age of AI reshapes our society. From the workplace to healthcare and education, AI alters the way we live and work. Job displacement prompts discussions on workforce reskilling and economic transformations. The ethical use of AI in criminal justice raises questions about fairness and accountability. The Age of AI invites us to rethink societal norms and values.

AI emerges as a powerful tool in addressing global challenges. Climate modeling powered by AI enhances our understanding of environmental changes. AI-driven energy optimization reduces carbon footprints. The Age of AI aligns with efforts to combat climate change and promote sustainability.

AI's presence in popular culture—depicted in films, books, and media—shapes public perception. It fuels fascination and apprehension, sparking discussions about AI's potential and risks. The Age of AI in popular culture reflects our collective imagination and apprehension about the future.

The Age of AI represents a transformative epoch in human history. It is a time of unparalleled technological innovation, ethical considerations, and societal change. As AI continues to advance, its impact on industries, economies, and societies worldwide is profound. Navigating this new era requires a thoughtful and ethical approach, one that harnesses the power of AI while addressing its challenges.

Chapter One: The AI Revolution Begins

In the preceding chapter, we ventured through time, tracing the origins of artificial intelligence (AI) from the dreams of ancient mythologies to the theoretical underpinnings of modern computing. As we step into the present, the stage is set for the AI revolution to unfold before our eyes—a revolution that promises to reshape industries, redefine our daily lives, and challenge the boundaries of what machines can achieve.

The Birth of Practical AI

The seeds of AI were sown in theoretical and philosophical musings, but it was in the second half of the 20th century that AI transitioned from abstract concepts to practical applications. This shift was marked by the development of early AI programs and the emergence of machines capable of problem-solving and decision-making.

Machine Learning and the Turing Test

At the core of AI's evolution was the concept of machine learning. Machine learning algorithms enable computers to analyze data, recognize patterns, and make predictions—an essential step toward artificial intelligence. One pivotal moment in AI history was the introduction of the Turing Test by Alan Turing in 1950, which proposed a way to measure a machine's ability to exhibit human-like intelligence in conversation.

Expert Systems and Rule-Based AI

The 1970s and 80s witnessed the rise of expert systems—AI programs designed to emulate the decision-making abilities of human experts in specific domains. These systems were based on rule-based AI, where explicit rules and knowledge were encoded into software. Expert systems found applications in fields like medicine, finance, and engineering, offering valuable insights and assistance to professionals.

AI Winter and Resurgence

Despite early promise, AI experienced a period known as the "AI winter" in the 1970s and 80s, marked by waning interest and funding due to unrealistic expectations and limited progress. However, this setback proved temporary. In the late 20th century, AI experienced a resurgence driven by advances in machine learning, neural networks, and the availability of more substantial computing power.

The Rise of Machine Learning and Deep Learning

Machine learning, particularly supervised learning, became a cornerstone of AI research. Algorithms like decision trees, support vector machines, and neural networks found applications in image and speech recognition, natural language processing, and data analysis. Deep learning, a subset of machine learning inspired by the structure and function of the human brain, ushered in remarkable breakthroughs, particularly in areas like computer vision and natural language understanding.

AI in the Digital Age

The digital age saw the proliferation of AI-driven technologies in our daily lives. Voice-activated virtual assistants like Siri, Google Assistant, and Alexa have become ubiquitous, offering us conversational interfaces to access information, control devices, and perform tasks. Recommendation systems powered by AI algorithms revolutionized how we discover content, from movies and music to books and products.

AI in Healthcare and Medicine

One of the most promising and transformative applications of AI can be found in healthcare. AI-driven diagnostic tools and predictive analytics are revolutionizing disease detection and personalized treatment plans. Machine learning models can analyze medical images with remarkable accuracy, aiding in early cancer detection and diagnostic precision.

AI in Finance and Economics

AI's impact on the financial sector has been profound. Algorithmic trading systems use AI to analyze market data and execute trades at speeds unattainable by human traders. Chatbots and virtual financial advisors provide personalized financial advice and assistance. Risk assessment and fraud detection have also benefited from AI's capabilities, making financial transactions more secure and efficient.

AI in Transportation and Autonomous Vehicles

The transportation industry is experiencing a seismic shift driven by AI. Companies like Tesla, Waymo, and Uber are pioneering self-driving cars that have the potential to revolutionize mobility by reducing accidents, congestion, and the need for parking spaces. AI-driven predictive maintenance systems are helping transportation companies reduce downtime and improve the reliability of their vehicles.

AI in Education and Personalized Learning

AI's influence in education is expanding rapidly. Adaptive learning platforms use AI to tailor educational content to individual students' needs, improving engagement and learning outcomes. Natural language processing and sentiment analysis are employed to evaluate and enhance written assignments and essays, providing students with constructive feedback.

AI in Scientific Discovery and Research

AI is accelerating scientific discovery by analyzing vast datasets and simulating complex phenomena. Genomics, drug discovery, and climate science are benefiting from AI's ability to process and interpret data at scales and speeds unattainable by human researchers. AI-driven simulations and modeling are transforming our understanding of the natural world.

AI's Role in Society and Challenges Ahead

As AI's influence continues to expand, it brings with it a host of societal questions and challenges. Issues of bias and fairness in AI algorithms, privacy concerns, and the ethical use of AI are becoming central topics of discussion. Ethical and moral dimensions of AI are critical aspects of its continued development and deployment and will shape the course of our human AI future.

The AI revolution has indeed begun, but it is a journey that is far from complete. In the chapters that follow, we will continue to explore the evolving landscape of AI, examining not only its technical intricacies but also its profound societal and ethical implications. The boundaries between science fiction and reality continue to blur, and the age of AI is no longer a distant fantasy but a remarkable and challenging reality.

The Historical Context of AI

Before we dive deeper into the contemporary landscape of artificial intelligence (AI), it's crucial to anchor ourselves in the historical context that gave birth to this revolutionary field. The story of AI is one of human fascination with the idea of creating intelligent machines, a fascination that stretches back through millennia.

Ancient Myths and Mechanical Marvels

The roots of AI can be traced to ancient civilizations and myths. In ancient Greece, for instance, tales of automatons and animated statues captured the human imagination. The myth of Pygmalion, a sculptor who fell in love with a statue he created and later brought to life, embodies the idea of creating lifelike beings from inanimate matter. These myths foreshadowed humanity's enduring fascination with the concept of artificial life.

Similarly, in ancient China, there are references to mechanical men and automata. These early conceptions of human-like machines reflected the human desire to craft beings that could mimic human actions and behaviors.

The Enlightenment and Mechanical Automata

The Enlightenment era marked a resurgence of interest in mechanical automata. Innovators like Jacques de Vaucanson and Pierre Jaquet-Droz created intricate clockwork automata that could perform remarkably complex movements and actions. Vaucanson's mechanical duck, which could eat, digest, and excrete food, captured the imagination of the era and showcased the potential for machines to emulate living creatures.

Charles Babbage and the Analytical Engine

The 19th century brought us closer to the dawn of computing with the work of Charles Babbage. Babbage designed the Analytical Engine, a mechanical computer that employed punch cards for programming.

Although the Analytical Engine was never built during Babbage's lifetime, it laid the theoretical foundation for modern computing by introducing concepts like stored programs and loops.

Alan Turing and the Turing Machine

The true birth of AI can be attributed to the genius of Alan Turing in the early 20th century. Turing's pioneering work in computer science and cryptography during World War II laid the foundation for AI. His concept of the Turing machine, a theoretical model of computation, demonstrated that any mathematical algorithm could be computed by a machine. This groundbreaking idea established the equivalence of human thought processes and computation—a concept fundamental to AI.

The Dartmouth Workshop and the Emergence of AI as a Field

The late 1950s marked a pivotal moment in the history of AI with the Dartmouth Workshop in 1956. This seminal event, organized by John McCarthy, Marvin Minsky, Nathaniel Rochester, and Claude Shannon, is considered the birth of AI as a formal field of study. It brought together computer scientists, mathematicians, and visionaries to explore the potential of machines that could mimic human intelligence.

Early AI Programs and Expert Systems

The post-Dartmouth era saw the development of early AI programs and the rise of expert systems. Researchers like Allen Newell and Herbert A. Simon created the Logic Theorist program, which could prove mathematical theorems. Expert systems, which aimed to replicate the decision-making abilities of human experts in specific domains, found applications in fields such as medicine, finance, and engineering.

AI Winters and Resurgence

Despite initial optimism, the field of AI experienced "AI winters" in the 1970s and 80s. These were periods of reduced funding and interest due to overinflated expectations and limited progress. However, AI experienced a resurgence in the late 20th century, fueled by advances in machine learning, neural networks, and the availability of more substantial computing power.

Contemporary AI and the Digital Age

Today, we find ourselves in an era where AI is deeply integrated into our lives. From voice-activated virtual assistants to recommendation algorithms, AI touches nearly every aspect of our digital existence. It's transforming industries, enabling scientific breakthroughs, and raising profound ethical questions about its use and impact.

As we continue our exploration of AI, we must keep this historical context in mind. AI is not an isolated phenomenon but the culmination of centuries of human fascination with the idea of creating intelligent machines. The AI revolution we're witnessing today is the latest chapter in this long and remarkable journey, and it is redefining the very boundaries of what machines can achieve.

Milestones in AI Development

The journey of artificial intelligence (AI) is paved with remarkable milestones—crucial turning points that have shaped and defined the field. These milestones represent the relentless human quest to create machines with the ability to think, learn, and exhibit intelligence. In this chapter, we delve into some of the most pivotal milestones in the development of AI.

1. The Turing Test (1950)

In 1950, the British mathematician and computer scientist Alan Turing introduced the concept of the Turing Test in his seminal paper, "Computing Machinery and Intelligence." This groundbreaking idea proposed a practical method for assessing a machine's capacity to demonstrate human-like intelligence through natural language conversation. While the Turing Test remains a subject of ongoing debate and refinement, it set an enduring standard for evaluating AI systems' competence in tasks involving human interaction, marking a fundamental step in AI history.

2. Logic Theorist (1956)

The Logic Theorist, developed by Allen Newell and Herbert A. Simon in 1956, represented a significant leap in early AI development. This pioneering program showcased AI's potential to solve complex mathematical problems by employing logical reasoning and rule-based algorithms. The Logic Theorist's success laid the foundation for future AI research in problem-solving and logical deduction, underscoring AI's capabilities beyond mere calculation.

3. Dartmouth Workshop (1956)

The Dartmouth Workshop, convened by John McCarthy, Marvin Minsky, Nathaniel Rochester, and Claude Shannon in the summer of 1956, holds a hallowed place in AI history. This historic gathering is regarded as the birth of AI as a formal academic field. It was during this event that the term "artificial intelligence" was coined, and the groundwork for dedicated AI research was laid. The Dartmouth Workshop marks the inception of systematic exploration into the potential and limitations of AI.

4. The General Problem Solver (1957)

Allen Newell and Herbert A. Simon further solidified their influence in AI development with the creation of the General Problem Solver (GPS) in 1957. GPS demonstrated AI's versatility by addressing a wide array of problems through heuristic problem-solving techniques. This program not only exemplified AI's problem-solving capabilities but also paved the way for the development of expert systems and other AI applications across various domains.

5. The Perceptron (1957)

In 1957, Frank Rosenblatt introduced the perceptron, an early form of a neural network model. Although limited in its ability to solve only linearly separable problems, the perceptron represented a crucial milestone in AI. It laid the foundation for subsequent developments in artificial neural networks, ultimately leading to the emergence of deep learning—a transformative breakthrough in AI that would revolutionize areas like image recognition and natural language understanding.

6. ELIZA (1966)

Joseph Weizenbaum's creation of ELIZA in 1966 marked a significant advance in AI's ability to engage in natural language conversation. ELIZA, often considered one of the first chatbots or conversational agents, simulated conversations with a Rogerian psychotherapist. It demonstrated how machines could interact with humans in a conversational manner, foreshadowing the development of modern conversational AI systems and chatbots.

7. Expert Systems (1970s-80s)

The 1970s and 80s witnessed the emergence of expert systems, a class of AI programs designed to replicate the decision-making abilities of human experts within specific domains. Dendral, an expert system for chemical analysis, and MYCIN, used for medical diagnosis, were notable examples. Expert systems found practical applications in diverse fields, from healthcare to finance, offering valuable insights and guidance in specialized areas.

8. The AI Winter (1970s-80s)

The AI winter, a period of reduced funding and waning interest in AI research during the 1970s and 80s, serves as a cautionary tale in AI history. It was characterized by overly optimistic expectations and limited progress, leading to skepticism about the field's feasibility. This era prompted a reevaluation of AI research priorities, ultimately contributing to a more grounded and pragmatic approach to AI development.

9. Deep Learning Resurgence (2000s)

The early 2000s witnessed a resurgence of interest in neural networks and deep learning. Advancements in hardware, particularly Graphics Processing Units (GPUs), and the availability of vast datasets revitalized neural network research. Deep learning models, including convolutional neural networks (CNNs) and recurrent neural networks (RNNs), achieved remarkable success in complex tasks such as image recognition and natural language processing. This resurgence heralded a new era of AI capabilities and applications.

10. AlphaGo (2016)

In 2016, DeepMind's AlphaGo made history by defeating the world champion Go player, Lee Sedol. This remarkable achievement showcased AI's ability to excel in complex games and reinforced learning, a subset of machine learning. AlphaGo employed deep neural networks and reinforcement learning algorithms to master the ancient and highly complex board game of Go. Its victory highlighted the potential of AI to tackle intricate decision-making tasks.

These milestones are not merely historical markers but key moments in the ongoing narrative of AI development. Each breakthrough represents a testament to human ingenuity, innovation, and the unrelenting pursuit of creating machines that can think and learn. As we navigate the evolving landscape of AI, these milestones continue to shape the trajectory of AI research and application, guiding us toward an ever-expanding horizon of possibilities.

AI's Impact on Various Industries

Artificial intelligence (AI) has transcended its theoretical origins to become a transformative force across numerous industries. Its ability to process vast amounts of data, recognize patterns, and make data-driven decisions has revolutionized the way businesses operate, leading to increased efficiency, productivity, and innovation. In this chapter, we explore the profound impact of AI on various industries.

Healthcare

AI has made significant inroads in the healthcare sector. Machine learning algorithms can analyze medical images with unparalleled accuracy, aiding in the early detection of diseases like cancer and facilitating personalized treatment plans. Natural language processing (NLP) powers chatbots and virtual assistants that assist in patient engagement and healthcare administration. Predictive analytics helps in optimizing resource allocation, and patient outcomes, and reducing healthcare costs.

Finance and Banking

AI has transformed the financial industry by automating tasks, enhancing fraud detection, and improving customer experiences. Algorithmic trading systems leverage AI to analyze market data and execute high-speed trades. Chatbots and virtual financial advisors provide personalized financial advice and assistance. AI-driven risk assessment models enhance lending decisions, making transactions more secure and efficient.

Transportation and Automotive
The transportation industry has seen a seismic shift driven by AI. Companies like Tesla, Waymo, and Uber are pioneering self-driving cars that have the potential to revolutionize mobility by reducing accidents, congestion, and the need for parking spaces. AI-powered predictive maintenance systems improve vehicle reliability and reduce downtime. Route optimization algorithms enhance logistics and supply chain management.

Education

AI is reshaping education through personalized learning experiences. Adaptive learning platforms use AI to tailor educational content to individual students' needs, improving engagement and learning outcomes. Natural language processing and sentiment analysis assist in evaluating written assignments and essays, providing students with constructive feedback. AI-driven educational tools are making learning more accessible and effective.

Retail

AI has revitalized the retail industry by providing personalized shopping experiences and optimizing supply chains. Recommendation systems powered by AI algorithms analyze customer data to suggest products tailored to individual preferences. Inventory management systems use predictive analytics to reduce waste and ensure products are always in stock. Computer vision and cashier-less technology are redefining the checkout process.

Manufacturing

Manufacturing processes have become more efficient and cost-effective with the integration of AI. Predictive maintenance systems leverage AI to anticipate machinery failures and reduce downtime. Robotic process automation (RPA) streamlines repetitive tasks, improving production efficiency. AI-powered quality control systems identify defects and ensure product consistency.

Entertainment and Media

AI is enhancing the entertainment and media industry by personalizing content recommendations and generating creative assets. Streaming platforms use AI to recommend movies, music, and shows based on user preferences and viewing habits. Content creation is augmented by AI-driven tools, automating tasks such as video editing and music composition.

Energy and Utilities

AI plays a vital role in optimizing energy consumption, grid management, and renewable energy integration. AI-powered smart grids balance supply and demand more efficiently, reducing energy wastage. Predictive maintenance of energy infrastructure minimizes downtime. Machine learning models forecast energy demand patterns, enabling better resource allocation.

Agriculture

AI is modernizing agriculture through precision farming techniques. AI-driven drones and sensors monitor crop health and provide real-time data on soil conditions. Machine learning algorithms analyze this data to optimize irrigation, pest control, and crop harvesting. AI-powered robots are used for planting and harvesting crops, increasing efficiency and reducing labor costs.

Aerospace and Defense

In the aerospace and defense sectors, AI is enhancing navigation, surveillance, and threat detection capabilities. AI-driven systems improve aircraft autopilots and autonomous drones. Predictive maintenance ensures military equipment remains mission-ready. AI algorithms analyze data from radar and satellites to identify potential threats.

AI's impact extends beyond these industries, permeating nearly every facet of modern life. As AI continues to evolve and mature, its influence will only grow, leading to further innovations and transformations in industries yet to be imagined. The synergy between human intelligence and artificial intelligence promises to redefine the boundaries of what is possible, ushering in a new era of innovation and discovery across diverse sectors.

Chapter Two: Understanding Artificial Intelligence

To grasp the significance and implications of artificial intelligence (AI), it's essential to delve into the foundational principles, key concepts, and underlying technologies that define this rapidly evolving field. In this chapter, we embark on a journey to understand AI, from its fundamental building blocks to its broader implications for society and our human future.

What is Artificial Intelligence?

At its core, AI seeks to create intelligent machines that can perform tasks typically requiring human intelligence. This encompasses a wide range of capabilities, from problem-solving and reasoning to perception and language understanding. AI systems aim to mimic and, in some cases, surpass human cognitive functions.

Machine Learning: The Heart of AI

Machine learning is a subset of AI that empowers systems to learn from data and improve their performance over time without explicit programming. It relies on algorithms and statistical models to recognize patterns, make predictions, and automate decision-making.

Types of AI

AI can be categorized into two primary types: Narrow or Weak AI and General or Strong AI. Narrow AI is designed for specific tasks, such as speech recognition or image classification. General AI, which remains a theoretical goal, would possess human-like intelligence and adaptability, capable of performing any intellectual task.

Supervised, Unsupervised, and Reinforcement Learning

Machine learning algorithms can be classified into different learning paradigms. Supervised learning involves training models on labeled data to make predictions. Unsupervised learning finds patterns in unlabeled data. Reinforcement learning employs reward-based mechanisms to optimize decision-making in dynamic environments.

Neural Networks and Deep Learning

Neural networks, inspired by the structure and function of the human brain, are a critical component of modern AI. Deep learning, a subset of neural networks, uses multiple layers to extract hierarchical features from data. It has led to breakthroughs in image recognition, natural language processing, and speech synthesis.

Natural Language Processing (NLP)

NLP enables computers to understand, interpret, and generate human language. It encompasses tasks like sentiment analysis, language translation, and chatbot interactions. Advances in NLP have transformed communication between humans and machines.

Computer Vision

Computer vision endows machines with the ability to interpret visual information from the world. AI-driven image recognition and object detection have applications in autonomous vehicles, medical imaging, and security systems.

AI Ethics and Bias

As AI becomes increasingly integrated into society, ethical considerations are paramount. Concerns related to bias in AI algorithms, data privacy, transparency, and accountability are at the forefront of discussions. Ethical AI development and responsible AI usage are essential for ensuring AI benefits society without reinforcing existing biases or harming marginalized groups.

The Future of AI

The future of AI holds exciting possibilities and challenges. It includes the development of more capable and adaptable AI systems, the exploration of human-AI collaboration, and ethical guidelines for AI research and deployment. The synergy between human intelligence and AI is poised to redefine industries, healthcare, education, and more.

The Role of AI in Our Lives

AI is no longer confined to the realm of research labs; it has permeated our daily lives. Voice-activated assistants, recommendation algorithms, and autonomous vehicles are just a few examples of how AI enhances convenience and efficiency. Understanding AI is crucial for navigating this AI-driven world effectively.

As we navigate this chapter, we embark on a voyage to comprehend AI's inner workings, its historical journey, and its potential to shape our human future. With this knowledge, we can engage with AI technologies more meaningfully, contribute to responsible AI development, and explore the boundless opportunities it presents for our society and the world at large.

Defining AI and Its Various Forms

Artificial intelligence (AI) is a dynamic and multifaceted field that encompasses a wide spectrum of technologies and applications. To truly understand AI's breadth and potential, we must first explore its core definition and the various forms it takes. In this chapter, we embark on a journey to define AI and shed light on its diverse manifestations.

The Essence of Artificial Intelligence

At its essence, AI seeks to imbue machines with human-like intelligence. This encompasses the capacity to perceive and interpret the world, reason and make decisions, learn from experience, and interact with humans in natural ways. AI endeavors to replicate and, in some cases, transcend the cognitive functions that define human intelligence.

The Continuum of AI Forms

AI is not a monolithic entity but rather a continuum of capabilities and technologies, each serving distinct purposes. Understanding the different forms of AI is crucial to appreciate the field's complexity and evolution.

Narrow or Weak AI

Narrow AI, often referred to as Weak AI, is designed to excel in specific tasks or domains. These AI systems are specialized experts, highly proficient within a defined context. Examples include virtual assistants like Siri or Alexa, chatbots for customer support, and recommendation algorithms that personalize content.

General or Strong AI

General AI, or Strong AI, represents the pinnacle of AI aspiration—a machine capable of emulating human intelligence across a broad range of tasks and domains. It possesses not only expertise but also adaptability, problem-solving abilities, and creativity akin to human cognition. While General AI remains a theoretical ideal, it serves as an inspiration and long-term objective for AI research.

Machine Learning and Statistical AI

Machine learning is a foundational component of AI, enabling machines to learn from data and improve their performance over time. It encompasses a variety of techniques, including supervised learning, unsupervised learning, and reinforcement learning. Machine learning algorithms form the basis for many AI applications, such as image recognition, natural language processing, and recommendation systems.

Neural Networks and Deep Learning

Neural networks, inspired by the human brain's structure, have emerged as a dominant paradigm in AI. Deep learning, a subset of neural networks, employs multiple layers to process data hierarchically, enabling the extraction of complex features from raw inputs. Deep learning has revolutionized fields like computer vision, speech recognition, and language understanding.

Natural Language Processing (NLP)

NLP is a specialized branch of AI focused on enabling machines to understand, interpret, and generate human language. NLP technologies underpin applications like language translation, sentiment analysis, chatbots, and voice assistants. They facilitate human-computer communication, making interactions more intuitive and accessible.

Computer Vision

Computer vision equips machines with the ability to interpret visual information from the world. AI-driven image recognition, object detection, and video analysis have applications in autonomous vehicles, healthcare diagnostics, facial recognition, and surveillance systems.

Robotics and Autonomous Systems

AI's integration with robotics has led to the development of autonomous systems capable of perceiving their environments and making decisions in real time. These systems have applications in manufacturing, healthcare, agriculture, and space exploration, among others.

The Intersection of AI and Ethics

AI's various forms raise ethical considerations. Issues of bias, transparency, accountability, and data privacy are central to AI ethics. Understanding these ethical dimensions is essential for ensuring responsible AI development and deployment.

The Future of AI Forms

As AI continues to advance, its forms will evolve and expand. This includes the development of AI systems with greater adaptability, problem-solving abilities, and ethical safeguards. The synergy between human intelligence and AI holds the promise of reshaping industries, enhancing healthcare, revolutionizing education, and addressing complex global challenges.

In this chapter, we embark on a journey through the diverse forms of AI, from Narrow AI specialized in specific tasks to the theoretical aspirations of General AI. This exploration serves as a foundation for our deeper understanding of AI's impact on society, its ethical considerations, and its potential to redefine our human future.

Machine Learning, Deep Learning, and Neural Networks

In the intricate landscape of artificial intelligence (AI), three foundational pillars have emerged as the driving forces behind its capabilities and innovations: machine learning, deep learning, and neural networks. In this chapter, we delve into the essence of these concepts, exploring how they underpin AI's evolution and shape the technology landscape.

Machine Learning: The Learning Paradigm

At the heart of AI lies machine learning, a paradigm that empowers machines to learn from data and improve their performance without explicit programming. Machine learning systems use algorithms and statistical models to recognize patterns, make predictions, and automate decision-making. Key components include:

- Supervised Learning: This method involves training models on labeled data, where the correct answers are provided. The model learns to make predictions based on input data and adjusts its parameters to minimize errors.

- Unsupervised Learning: In unsupervised learning, machines analyze unlabeled data to discover patterns and structures independently. This method is often used for tasks like clustering and dimensionality reduction.

- Reinforcement Learning: Reinforcement learning employs a reward-based approach, where agents learn by taking actions in an environment and receiving feedback in the form of rewards or penalties. It's crucial for tasks requiring sequential decision-making.

Deep Learning: Unleashing the Neural Power

Deep learning is a subfield of machine learning that has garnered immense attention and achieved groundbreaking results. At its core, deep learning leverages neural networks, which are inspired by the structure and function of the human brain. These networks consist of layers of interconnected nodes, or neurons, and excel in processing vast amounts of data with hierarchical features. Key aspects of deep learning include:

- Neural Networks: Neural networks are composed of interconnected layers of neurons, each layer extracting increasingly abstract features from data. The depth of these networks allows them to learn complex representations, making them exceptionally suited for tasks like image recognition and natural language processing.

- Convolutional Neural Networks (CNNs): CNNs are specialized neural networks designed for image analysis. They use convolutional layers to identify local patterns in images, enabling precise object detection and recognition.

- Recurrent Neural Networks (RNNs): RNNs are well-suited for sequential data and tasks involving temporal dependencies. They maintain internal states, enabling them to process sequences of variable length. RNNs are widely used in tasks like natural language generation and speech recognition.

Neural Networks: The Building Blocks of Intelligence

Neural networks are the fundamental building blocks of deep learning. These computational models mimic the interconnected structure of neurons in the human brain. Neural networks consist of layers, including an input layer, one or more hidden layers, and an output layer. Each neuron processes information and passes it on to subsequent layers. This hierarchical structure allows neural networks to learn complex patterns and representations from data.

- Activation Functions: Neurons within neural networks use activation functions to introduce non-linearity into the model, enabling them to capture complex relationships in data.

- Backpropagation: Training neural networks involves an iterative process called backpropagation, where errors are propagated backward through the network. This process adjusts the model's parameters to minimize errors and improve performance.

- Deep Neural Networks: Deep learning takes neural networks to new heights by stacking multiple hidden layers, creating deep neural networks. This architecture allows them to learn intricate features and representations, leading to remarkable breakthroughs in AI.

In this chapter, we've unraveled the core concepts of machine learning, deep learning, and neural networks—the bedrock upon which AI innovation thrives. These technologies have revolutionized industries, empowered intelligent systems, and paved the way for AI's continued evolution. As we proceed, we'll explore how these concepts are harnessed to drive practical applications and shape the AI landscape.

The Role of Data in AI

In the realm of artificial intelligence (AI), data is not merely a resource; it's the lifeblood that fuels intelligence, informs decision-making, and enables learning. Understanding the pivotal role of data in AI is paramount. In this chapter, we dive deep into the significance of data and its transformative impact on AI applications.

Data as the Foundation

At its core, AI is about making sense of data. The more data an AI system has access to, the more informed its decisions and predictions become. Data serves as the raw material from which AI extracts patterns, insights, and knowledge. Whether it's text, images, audio, or sensor data, the diversity of data types enriches AI's capabilities.

Data Collection and Preparation

The process of gathering, cleaning, and organizing data is a critical precursor to AI success. High-quality data is essential for training machine learning models effectively. This involves removing noise, dealing with missing values, and ensuring data consistency. Ethical considerations, such as data privacy and consent, also play a significant role in the data preparation phase.

Training AI Models

Machine learning models, at their core, learn from data. During the training process, AI models analyze labeled data, learning to recognize patterns and associations. The more diverse and representative the training data, the better the model's generalization to unseen data. The process often involves splitting data into training, validation, and test sets to evaluate model performance.

Supervised Learning and Labeled Data

In supervised learning, AI models are trained on labeled data, where each example is paired with the correct answer or target. This pairing allows the model to learn and generalize from the provided labels. Applications include image classification, language translation, and sentiment analysis.

Unsupervised Learning and Unlabeled Data

Unsupervised learning, on the other hand, leverages unlabeled data to discover patterns and structures independently. Clustering algorithms group similar data points, while dimensionality reduction techniques simplify complex data representations. Unsupervised learning is valuable for tasks like customer segmentation and anomaly detection.

The Value of Big Data

The era of big data has ushered in a new paradigm for AI. With vast volumes of data generated daily, AI systems have access to a wealth of information. Big data analytics and AI's data-processing capabilities have transformed industries like finance, healthcare, and marketing. The ability to extract insights from massive datasets enables data-driven decision-making and innovation.

Real-time Data and IoT

The Internet of Things (IoT) has added another dimension to AI by providing a continuous stream of real-time data from sensors and devices. AI systems can process this data to make immediate decisions and predictions, with applications ranging from smart homes to industrial automation.

Ethical Considerations

As data is central to AI's operation, ethical concerns surrounding data usage are paramount. Issues such as data privacy, bias in datasets, and responsible data collection and storage demand careful attention. Ethical AI development ensures that AI systems respect individual rights and societal values.

Data-Driven Innovation

AI's power to harness data extends beyond traditional industries. It is driving innovation in areas like personalized medicine, autonomous vehicles, recommendation systems, and language processing. These innovations are changing the way we live, work, and interact with technology.

The Future of Data in AI

The role of data in AI is continually evolving. Advancements in data collection, storage, and processing technologies will empower AI systems to handle even larger and more complex datasets. Data ethics and responsible AI practices will become increasingly important as AI's reach expands into new domains.

In this chapter, we've unveiled the pivotal role of data in AI's functioning and growth. Data, in its myriad forms, fuels AI's learning, decision-making, and transformative potential. As we progress through this exploration of AI, we'll witness how data-driven insights and innovations shape our increasingly intelligent and interconnected world.

Chapter Three: From Sci-Fi to Reality

The transition of artificial intelligence (AI) from the realm of science fiction to tangible reality is a remarkable journey that encapsulates the fusion of human imagination with technological innovation. In this chapter, we embark on an intriguing exploration of how AI, once a product of speculative fiction, has metamorphosed into a transformative force that is reshaping our world in profound ways.

The Early Visions of AI

The origins of AI can be traced back to the earliest human myths and tales featuring intelligent machines and automatons. However, it wasn't until the 20th century that AI emerged as a formal field of study, guided by visionaries like Alan Turing and John McCarthy. These pioneers laid the intellectual foundations for envisioning machines capable of emulating human cognition.

AI Winters and Resurgences

AI's history is marked by periods of exuberance followed by disappointments, often referred to as "AI winters." These episodes of dashed expectations were driven by the realization of the immense challenges in achieving human-level intelligence in machines. Nevertheless, AI persevered, and the late 20th century witnessed a resurgence, powered by advances in computing power and the maturation of machine learning.

Sci-Fi Inspirations

The realm of science fiction has been a wellspring of inspiration for AI researchers and enthusiasts alike. Works such as Isaac Asimov's "Robot" series, Arthur C. Clarke's enigmatic "HAL 9000," and Philip K. Dick's explorations of artificial consciousness have not only captivated audiences but also spurred real-world scientific inquiry, challenging societal perceptions of AI.

Realizing AI's Potential

Over time, the realm of possibility expanded as practical applications of AI materialized. Expert systems, natural language processing, and early forms of machine learning started to take shape. AI ceased to be a mere vision and became a tangible, problem-solving tool.

The Rise of Machine Learning

Machine learning, a subset of AI, emerged as a transformative force, propelling AI into new frontiers. This paradigm shift allowed machines to learn from data, extract patterns, and make predictions. It marked the beginning of AI's ability to excel in tasks such as image recognition, language translation, and autonomous decision-making.

Neural Networks and Deep Learning

The resurgence of AI can be largely attributed to the advent of neural networks and deep learning. These technologies, inspired by the intricate structure of the human brain, unlocked unprecedented capabilities. Deep learning, characterized by multiple layers of artificial neurons, revolutionized computer vision, natural language understanding, and complex problem-solving.

AI in Everyday Life

In the present day, AI is seamlessly woven into the fabric of our daily existence. Virtual assistants like Siri and Alexa provide personalized assistance, recommendation algorithms influence our entertainment choices, and autonomous vehicles are poised to redefine transportation. AI is ubiquitous, impacting industries ranging from healthcare to finance.

Ethical and Societal Considerations

The ascent of AI has ushered in a host of ethical and societal considerations. Discussions about fairness, transparency, and accountability in AI algorithms, alongside concerns about data privacy and AI's impact on the job market, have taken center stage. Striking a harmonious balance between AI's benefits and potential risks is a pressing challenge.

The Future of AI

The journey from sci-fi to reality is ongoing. As AI continues to advance, with breakthroughs in reinforcement learning, robotics, and quantum computing on the horizon, it promises a future where AI systems are not only intelligent but also ethical, explainable, and deeply aligned with human values.

The Intersection of Human Creativity and AI

One of the most exciting prospects of AI's evolution is its role as a catalyst for human creativity and innovation. Artists collaborate with AI to create unique works, scientists employ AI to accelerate research, and educators leverage AI for personalized learning experiences. The synergy between human ingenuity and AI's computational prowess opens the door to boundless possibilities.

In this chapter, we embark on a captivating journey that traces AI's transition from the pages of science fiction to the reality that surrounds us. We witness how AI has evolved, not only as a technological marvel but also as a potent force that is reshaping our world in ways once imagined only in the realms of speculative fiction.

Prominent AI in Pop Culture

AI's Presence in Science Fiction

The vast realm of science fiction literature and cinema has served as a rich playground for exploring the intricate tapestry of artificial intelligence (AI). It's here that we've encountered some of the most iconic AI characters and grappled with fundamental questions about the nature of consciousness and technology. In Isaac Asimov's seminal "Robot" series, we were introduced to the Three Laws of Robotics, which governed the behavior of intelligent humanoid robots and posed profound ethical dilemmas. Arthur C. Clarke's "HAL 9000" from "2001: A Space Odyssey" showcased the dangers of AI going rogue, forever etching into our collective consciousness the haunting refrain, "I'm sorry, Dave. I'm afraid I can't do that." These early depictions laid the foundation for our understanding of AI's potential, ethics, and consequences.

Redefining Sentience and Identity

AI has not merely been portrayed as a tool or a servant in science fiction but as a thought-provoking challenge to our understanding of sentience and identity. Films like "Blade Runner" thrust us into a dystopian world where bioengineered androids known as replicants blur the lines between human and machine. These narratives compel us to confront existential questions about what it truly means to be human and whether AI can genuinely attain consciousness and self-awareness. The enigmatic replicants invite us to ponder the ethical implications of creating entities that may share our desires, dreams, and vulnerabilities.

Friendly AI Companions

While some AI portrayals in pop culture emphasize the dangers and moral dilemmas, others offer a more heartwarming perspective. Characters like R2-D2 and C-3PO from the "Star Wars" franchise have endeared themselves to generations of fans as loyal and resourceful companions. Similarly, Wall-E, the endearing waste-collecting robot from Pixar's "Wall-E," tugs at our heartstrings and showcases the potential for

AI to be empathetic and charming companions. These AI characters demonstrate the multifaceted roles that AI can play, from providing comic relief to offering unwavering support and camaraderie.

AI as a Moral Compass

In the world of science fiction, AI often grapples with complex moral dilemmas, bringing to light the potential for AI to serve as a moral compass in ethically challenging situations. "I, Robot," inspired by Isaac Asimov's work, explores a future where AI robots adhere to a set of ethical guidelines known as the Three Laws of Robotics. Through the lens of these laws, the film raises thought-provoking questions about AI's role in upholding moral principles and navigating intricate ethical landscapes. These narratives remind us that AI when designed with ethical considerations in mind, has the potential to assist in making morally sound decisions, a capability that could prove invaluable in a world confronted with complex moral choices.

AI in Modern Cinema

Contemporary cinema continues to explore the intricacies of human-AI relationships, shedding light on the evolving dynamics between humans and AI in an increasingly digital world. Films like "Ex Machina" delve into the blurred lines between creator and creation as a young programmer interacts with a highly advanced AI housed in a humanoid robotic body. The film explores themes of deception, manipulation, and the inherent power dynamics in human-AI interactions. Similarly, "Her" explores the unconventional romantic relationship between a man and an AI operating system. The film explores the emotional connections that can develop between humans and AI, raising questions about intimacy, loneliness, and the boundaries of human-AI interactions. These modern cinematic masterpieces push the boundaries of storytelling and challenge our perceptions of the evolving role of AI in our lives.

AI in Video Games

The influence of AI is not confined to the silver screen but extends into the immersive world of video games. In this interactive medium, AI takes on diverse roles, from powering non-playable characters (NPCs) with advanced decision-making capabilities to challenging players as AI-driven opponents in competitive gaming. NPCs exhibit lifelike behaviors, responding to player actions and dynamically adapting to the game environment. AI in video games provides players with challenging adversaries and rich, interactive storytelling experiences, further blurring the line between reality and virtual worlds.

AI's Pop Culture Impact

The portrayal of AI in pop culture has had a profound impact on public perceptions and discussions surrounding AI ethics, safety, and human-AI interactions. These fictional narratives have sparked debates and conversations about the potential benefits and risks associated with AI. They have acted as a mirror reflecting our hopes, fears, and aspirations regarding the future of technology. As AI becomes an increasingly integral part of our reality, its portrayal in pop culture continues to influence our understanding of its potential and limitations.

Inspiring Real-World Innovation

Interestingly, the AI depicted in pop culture has often served as a wellspring of inspiration for real-world AI research and development. Researchers and engineers draw inspiration from fictional AI characters and scenarios to design and improve AI systems. Concepts such as natural language understanding, computer vision, and conversational agents have been propelled forward by the imaginative depictions of AI in literature and cinema. These real-world innovations bring us closer to realizing some of the fantastical AI visions that once seemed confined to the realm of fiction.

The Ongoing Influence of Pop Culture

As AI continues to evolve, pop culture remains a potent influencer in shaping public perceptions and driving conversations about AI's place in our rapidly changing world. New films, books, and entertainment offerings continue to explore AI's potential, pushing the boundaries of our imagination and challenging our assumptions about the future of technology. The ongoing interplay between AI in pop culture and AI in reality ensures that the dialogue about AI remains dynamic and relevant, stimulating our curiosity and shaping our technological journey.

In this chapter, we embark on a journey through the fascinating world of AI in pop culture. From iconic characters to thought-provoking narratives, we explore how AI has been depicted in movies, literature, and entertainment, and how these portrayals have both reflected and influenced our perceptions of this transformative technology.

Ethical and Philosophical Considerations

The ascent of artificial intelligence (AI) brings forth a multitude of ethical and philosophical considerations, challenging us to grapple with profound questions about the nature of intelligence, consciousness, autonomy, and the moral implications of creating intelligent entities. In this chapter, we embark on a contemplative journey into the heart of AI's ethical and philosophical dimensions, exploring the complex terrain where technology and human values intersect.

The Ethical Imperatives of AI

As AI evolves, the need for ethical guidelines and principles becomes increasingly urgent. Ethical considerations in AI encompass a wide array of issues, from ensuring fairness and transparency in algorithms to addressing biases in data and AI decision-making. Ethical frameworks aim to guide the development and deployment of AI in ways that align with human values and respect individual rights.

The Moral Status of AI

One of the central philosophical questions that AI raises is whether intelligent machines can possess a moral status. Does AI, when endowed with decision-making capabilities, deserve moral consideration, or are they mere tools created by humans? Exploring the moral dimensions of AI involves pondering questions about AI rights, responsibilities, and the implications of creating entities capable of moral judgment.

Autonomy and Responsibility

AI systems increasingly exhibit autonomy in decision-making, raising questions about where the line between human responsibility and AI responsibility should be drawn. When AI systems make decisions that impact human lives, who bears the moral and legal responsibility for those decisions? This ethical dilemma challenges traditional notions of accountability.

The Nature of Consciousness and Intelligence

Philosophers and scientists continue to debate whether AI can truly exhibit consciousness and intelligence akin to that of humans. The quest to define and understand consciousness leads us to explore the nature of self-awareness, subjective experience, and the potential for AI to possess genuine consciousness or mere simulations of it.

Bias, Fairness, and Discrimination

AI algorithms are only as unbiased as the data they are trained on. Ethical concerns arise when AI systems perpetuate or amplify biases present in training data, potentially leading to discriminatory outcomes. Addressing these biases requires ethical considerations at every stage of AI development, from data collection to model design and evaluation.

Privacy and Data Ethics

The vast amounts of data used to train and operate AI systems raise profound questions about privacy and data ethics. AI's ability to analyze and predict human behavior raises concerns about surveillance, data security, and the responsible handling of sensitive information. Ethical guidelines aim to protect individuals' privacy and data rights in an AI-driven world.

Ethical Decision-Making by AI

As AI systems become more autonomous, they are entrusted with making decisions that have ethical implications. Should AI prioritize human safety over other considerations, and how should AI weigh conflicting ethical principles? Developing ethical AI involves defining the criteria and values that guide AI decision-making.

The Trolley Problem and Moral Dilemmas

The famous ethical thought experiment known as the "trolley problem" takes on new dimensions in the context of AI-driven autonomous vehicles. How should AI systems make life-and-death decisions in situations where moral dilemmas arise? These scenarios force us to confront the challenges of programming AI to make ethically sound choices.

Human-AI Collaboration

The integration of AI into various aspects of society, including healthcare and criminal justice, raises questions about the ethical implications of human-AI collaboration. How do we ensure that AI augments human decision-making rather than undermining it, and how should AI be regulated in collaborative contexts?

The Role of Ethicists and Philosophers

Ethicists and philosophers play a crucial role in shaping the ethical discourse surrounding AI. Their contributions help us navigate the intricate landscape of AI ethics, providing frameworks, guidelines, and critical perspectives that inform responsible AI development and deployment.

The Ongoing Ethical Conversation

The ethical and philosophical considerations surrounding AI are dynamic and ongoing. As AI technologies continue to advance, ethical discussions adapt and evolve, reflecting new challenges and opportunities. The ongoing dialogue between AI practitioners, ethicists, philosophers, policymakers, and the wider public ensures that AI evolves in ways that align with human values and societal well-being.

In this chapter, we delve deep into the ethical and philosophical dimensions of AI, exploring the complex tapestry of values, principles, and moral quandaries that arise as technology intersects with human values. The ethical and philosophical discourse surrounding AI challenges us to navigate a path that harnesses AI's potential for good while safeguarding against its potential pitfalls, fostering a future where AI is not just intelligent but also ethically aligned with our shared values and aspirations.

Part II: The AI Landscape

In this chapter, we delve into the intricate and multifaceted terrain of the AI landscape. It represents a dynamic and evolving space characterized by rapid advancements, diverse applications, and profound implications across industries and society.

The AI ecosystem serves as a thriving hub for collaboration and innovation, encompassing a wide array of stakeholders, from researchers and developers to policymakers and businesses. This rich tapestry of contributors propels the development and dissemination of AI technologies, shaping their trajectory and impact.

The proliferation of AI technologies within this landscape extends far beyond traditional machine learning algorithms. It encompasses deep learning, reinforcement learning, natural language processing, computer vision, and more. These technologies serve as the driving force behind transformative applications in fields such as healthcare, finance, and marketing, redefining how industries operate and compete.

Moreover, startups and innovators play a vital role in this landscape. Emerging companies inject fresh ideas and solutions, often disrupting established industries and challenging the status quo. Venture capital flows into AI startups, nurturing innovation in areas such as robotics, AI ethics, and quantum computing.

Ethical and regulatory considerations take center stage as AI technologies become more ubiquitous. Privacy, bias, fairness, and transparency emerge as critical issues. Policymakers grapple with the task of striking a delicate balance between fostering innovation and safeguarding individual rights and interests.

In academia, research institutions and universities form the backbone of AI advancements. They conduct groundbreaking studies that push the boundaries of AI capabilities. Collaboration between academia and industry leads to the development of cutting-edge technologies, further enriching the AI landscape.

The AI landscape also significantly impacts the workforce. AI automation may displace certain jobs, necessitating reskilling and upskilling efforts. Simultaneously, it creates new opportunities in AI development, ethics, and maintenance, reshaping the nature of work in the AI-augmented world.

Global competition marks the landscape as nations and tech giants vie for leadership in AI research and development. Countries like the United States, China, and European nations invest heavily in AI, influencing economic and technological power dynamics on the world stage.

AI's potential for social good shines brightly within this landscape. It aids in disaster response, climate modeling, and public health, addressing critical global challenges. AI technologies promote sustainability and contribute to a more equitable and accessible world.

The AI landscape also permeates popular culture, shaping public perception and discourse. Portrayed in films, books, and media, AI fuels discussions about its potential and risks, inspiring both fascination and apprehension.

In conclusion, the AI landscape is a diverse, dynamic, and evolving ecosystem that encompasses technological innovation, ethical considerations, and societal transformation. It represents a complex interplay of forces that are reshaping industries, economies, and societies across the globe. Navigating this landscape requires a comprehensive understanding of its components and the ability to adapt to its continuous evolution.

Chapter Four: The Current State of AI

In the ever-evolving landscape of artificial intelligence (AI), it is crucial to pause and take stock of the current state of affairs. This chapter offers a comprehensive overview of where AI stands today, exploring the remarkable advancements, ongoing challenges, and the transformative impact AI is having across various domains.

The AI Ecosystem

The AI ecosystem is vast and dynamic, encompassing a multitude of subfields, technologies, and applications. At its core, AI revolves around the concept of machines exhibiting intelligent behavior. Machine learning, deep learning, natural language processing, and computer vision are among the key pillars of AI, each contributing to AI's versatility and adaptability.

The Role of Data

Data is the lifeblood of AI, and the current state of AI is intricately linked to the unprecedented availability and volume of data. AI algorithms learn from massive datasets, making predictions, recognizing patterns, and powering intelligent applications. Big data and data analytics are essential components of the AI landscape.

Deep Learning Dominance

Deep learning, a subset of machine learning, has been a driving force behind recent AI breakthroughs. Neural networks with multiple layers (deep neural networks) have proven highly effective in tasks such as image recognition, natural language understanding, and game-playing. Deep learning has enabled AI systems to achieve human-level performance in various domains.

AI in Healthcare

One of the most promising applications of AI is in healthcare. AI-powered diagnostic tools, predictive analytics, and personalized treatment recommendations are revolutionizing patient care. Machine learning models can analyze medical images, detect diseases, and assist in drug discovery, leading to more accurate diagnoses and improved outcomes.

AI in Finance

The financial industry relies heavily on AI for fraud detection, algorithmic trading, and risk assessment. AI models analyze vast financial datasets to identify anomalies and trends, making it possible to prevent fraudulent activities and optimize investment strategies.

AI in Natural Language Processing

Natural language processing (NLP) has made significant strides. AI systems can now understand and generate human language with remarkable accuracy. Virtual assistants like Siri and chatbots handle natural language queries, while AI-driven language translation services bridge linguistic gaps on a global scale.

AI in Autonomous Systems

Autonomous systems, including self-driving cars and drones, rely on AI algorithms to navigate and make real-time decisions. These technologies have the potential to transform transportation, logistics, and even urban planning.

AI in Entertainment and Creativity

AI has made inroads into the creative realm, with algorithms generating art, music, and literature. Machine learning models analyze artistic styles and create unique works, blurring the lines between human and AI-generated creativity.

AI Ethics and Bias Mitigation

As AI's influence grows, so do concerns about ethics and bias. The AI community is actively addressing these issues through research, guidelines, and regulatory efforts. Fairness, transparency, and accountability are central themes in AI ethics.

AI and the Workforce

The impact of AI on employment and the workforce is a topic of ongoing debate. While AI has the potential to automate certain tasks, it also creates new opportunities in AI development, maintenance, and oversight. The future of work is likely to involve close collaboration between humans and AI.

Challenges and Concerns

Despite its advancements, AI faces persistent challenges. Ensuring the privacy and security of data used by AI systems remains a top priority. The interpretability of AI decisions, particularly in high-stakes applications like healthcare and law, is another ongoing concern. Additionally, AI's energy consumption and environmental impact are subjects of scrutiny.

The Global AI Landscape

AI is a global phenomenon, with leading research and development hubs in countries such as the United States, China, and Europe. Collaboration and competition between nations in AI research, innovation, and policy are shaping the future of AI on a global scale.

Future Directions

The current state of AI is a dynamic snapshot of a field in constant flux. The future promises further advancements in AI, including developments in reinforcement learning, quantum computing, and ethical AI. AI's impact on industries, society, and human-machine collaboration will continue to expand, presenting both opportunities and challenges.

This chapter provides a comprehensive overview of the current state of AI, highlighting its pervasive influence across industries, its transformative potential, and the ethical considerations that accompany its growth. As AI continues to shape our world, staying informed about its current capabilities and future prospects is essential for understanding its role in our evolving society.

An Overview of Contemporary AI Technologies

In the fast-paced world of artificial intelligence (AI), a myriad of cutting-edge technologies is shaping our present and future. This chapter provides a detailed overview of the contemporary AI technologies that are driving innovation, transforming industries, and revolutionizing the way we interact with technology.

Machine Learning: The Foundation of AI

Machine learning serves as the bedrock of contemporary AI. It is a subfield of AI that focuses on the development of algorithms and models that enable systems to learn from data. Supervised learning, unsupervised learning, and reinforcement learning are the primary categories of machine learning. These algorithms empower AI systems to make predictions, recognize patterns, and improve performance through experience.

Deep Learning: The Power of Neural Networks

Deep learning, a subset of machine learning, has gained immense popularity and has proven to be a game-changer in various applications. Deep neural networks, inspired by the human brain's structure, consist of multiple layers (hence "deep") of interconnected artificial neurons. This architecture has driven breakthroughs in computer vision, natural language processing, and speech recognition. Convolutional neural networks (CNNs) excel in image analysis, while recurrent neural networks (RNNs) are adept at sequential data processing.

Natural Language Processing (NLP): Understanding Human Language

NLP is a subfield of AI that focuses on the interaction between computers and human language. Contemporary NLP models, such as transformer-based models, have achieved remarkable results in tasks like language translation, text generation, sentiment analysis, and question-answering. These models, fueled by vast amounts of data and computational power, have ushered in a new era of human-computer communication.

Computer Vision: Enabling Machines to See

Computer vision empowers machines to interpret and understand visual information from the world. Object detection, image segmentation, and facial recognition are among the applications of computer vision. AI-driven cameras, such as those in smartphones and autonomous vehicles, leverage computer vision to perceive their surroundings and make decisions.

Reinforcement Learning: Training AI through Interaction

Reinforcement learning is a paradigm of machine learning where AI agents learn to make sequences of decisions by interacting with an environment. It is instrumental in developing autonomous systems, such as self-driving cars and game-playing AI. Reinforcement learning algorithms aim to maximize a cumulative reward signal, making them well-suited for scenarios involving decision-making and exploration.

Generative Adversarial Networks (GANs): Creativity in AI

GANs are a class of AI models that consist of two neural networks, a generator, and a discriminator, engaged in a competitive learning process. GANs are renowned for their ability to generate highly realistic images, videos, and even text. They have found applications in art generation, deepfake creation, and data augmentation.

AI in Robotics: Bridging the Physical and Digital Worlds

AI is integral to the field of robotics, enabling robots to perform tasks ranging from manufacturing and healthcare to exploration and entertainment. Collaborative robots (cobots) work alongside humans in industrial settings, while autonomous drones and rovers explore remote environments. AI-driven advancements in robotic perception, planning, and control are pushing the boundaries of what robots can achieve.

Edge AI: Bringing Intelligence to the Edge

Edge AI is a growing trend that involves deploying AI algorithms directly on edge devices, such as smartphones, IoT devices, and edge servers. This approach reduces latency, enhances privacy, and conserves bandwidth by processing data locally. Edge AI enables real-time applications like voice assistants, facial recognition, and augmented reality.

AI in Healthcare: Transforming Diagnosis and Treatment

The healthcare industry has witnessed a surge in AI applications, from medical imaging and disease diagnosis to drug discovery and personalized treatment plans. AI models analyze medical images with remarkable accuracy, aiding radiologists in detecting diseases. Drug discovery pipelines benefit from AI-driven simulations and predictive analytics.

AI in Finance: Revolutionizing Financial Services

In the financial sector, AI is driving automation, fraud detection, risk assessment, and algorithmic trading. AI algorithms analyze market data, identify trading opportunities, and execute trades at speeds impossible for humans. Chatbots and virtual assistants are becoming commonplace in customer service, offering personalized financial advice.

AI in Natural Resource Management: Environmental Stewardship

AI technologies are increasingly used in natural resource management and environmental monitoring. AI-powered sensors and satellite imagery help track deforestation, manage water resources, and monitor wildlife populations. These applications aid in sustainable resource management and conservation efforts.

AI in Entertainment: Crafting Personalized Experiences

The entertainment industry harnesses AI to enhance user experiences. Streaming platforms use recommendation algorithms to suggest content, while AI-driven animation tools streamline the creative process. AI-generated music and art are expanding the boundaries of creativity and entertainment.

AI and Cybersecurity: Defending Against Threats

AI plays a crucial role in cybersecurity by identifying and mitigating threats in real time. AI-powered cybersecurity systems analyze network traffic, detect anomalies, and respond to cyberattacks. AI enhances threat detection and incident response, bolstering defenses against evolving cyber threats.

AI Ethics and Regulation: Ensuring Responsible Development

As AI technologies advance, concerns about ethics and regulation become increasingly relevant. Ensuring the ethical use of AI, addressing bias and discrimination, and establishing clear regulations are essential for responsible AI development.

AI and Quantum Computing: A Glimpse of the Future

The convergence of AI and quantum computing holds promise for solving complex problems that are currently beyond the reach of classical computing. Quantum AI algorithms have the potential to revolutionize optimization, cryptography, and material science.

This chapter offers a comprehensive overview of contemporary AI technologies that are at the forefront of innovation. These technologies are not only shaping the present but also laying the foundation for an AI-driven future where intelligent systems become increasingly integrated into our daily lives and industries.

AI in Healthcare: Revolutionizing Diagnosis and Treatment

AI is making profound strides in the healthcare sector, redefining how diseases are diagnosed, treated, and managed.

Medical Imaging: AI is transforming medical imaging by enhancing the accuracy and efficiency of diagnoses. Machine learning algorithms can analyze radiological images such as X-rays, MRIs, and CT scans, assisting radiologists in identifying anomalies, tumors, and fractures. This not only reduces the time needed for diagnosis but also improves the overall accuracy, ultimately leading to better patient outcomes.

Drug Discovery: AI is accelerating drug discovery by streamlining the identification of potential compounds. Machine learning models can predict the biological activity of molecules, significantly reducing the time and cost required for drug development. AI-driven simulations and virtual drug screening have become indispensable tools in pharmaceutical research.

Personalized Medicine: AI enables the practice of personalized medicine by analyzing patient data to tailor treatments to individual genetic, lifestyle, and health factors. This approach enhances treatment efficacy and minimizes adverse effects. Genomic sequencing and AI-powered predictive analytics are at the forefront of this transformation.

Telemedicine and Remote Monitoring: Telemedicine, amplified by AI, provides remote healthcare services, connecting patients with healthcare professionals through digital platforms. AI-driven chatbots and virtual assistants can assist with symptom assessment and scheduling appointments. Remote monitoring devices equipped with AI algorithms track vital signs, enabling early detection of health issues and reducing hospital readmissions.

Disease Prediction and Prevention: AI can analyze vast datasets to predict disease outbreaks and epidemics. Machine learning models can identify disease risk factors and patterns, helping public health organizations allocate resources efficiently. Additionally, AI can assist in early disease detection, such as diabetic retinopathy screening using retinal images.

AI in Finance: Enhancing Efficiency and Risk Management

The financial industry is leveraging AI to optimize operations, improve risk assessment, and enhance customer experiences.

Algorithmic Trading: AI algorithms analyze vast amounts of financial data at lightning speed, executing trades based on predefined criteria and real-time market conditions. These algorithms outperform human traders in terms of speed and precision, and they can uncover hidden trading opportunities.

Risk Assessment: AI models assess credit risk, investment risk, and market risk more accurately than traditional methods. They analyze historical data, market trends, and economic indicators to provide more informed risk assessments. This reduces the likelihood of financial crises and enhances investment strategies.

Fraud Detection: AI-powered fraud detection systems use machine learning to identify suspicious transactions and behaviors. These systems continuously monitor financial transactions, flagging potentially fraudulent activities and protecting both financial institutions and customers from fraudulent attacks.

Customer Service: Chatbots and virtual assistants powered by AI provide 24/7 customer support. They can answer inquiries, assist with account management, and provide personalized financial advice. This enhances customer satisfaction and reduces operational costs for financial institutions.

Quantitative Analysis: AI-driven quantitative analysis helps financial analysts and asset managers make data-driven decisions. Machine learning models analyze vast datasets, uncovering investment opportunities and optimizing portfolio management.

AI in Transportation: Paving the Way for Mobility

AI is reshaping transportation by improving safety, efficiency, and sustainability in various modes of transportation.

Autonomous Vehicles: Self-driving cars and autonomous trucks are at the forefront of AI in transportation. AI algorithms process data from sensors, cameras, and lidar to navigate roads, make real-time decisions, and enhance road safety. Autonomous vehicles have the potential to reduce accidents, traffic congestion, and fuel consumption.

Traffic Management: AI is used in traffic management systems to optimize traffic flow, reduce congestion, and improve road safety. Adaptive traffic signals, powered by AI, adjust signal timings in response to real-time traffic conditions, minimizing delays and idling times.

Predictive Maintenance: In aviation and rail transportation, AI is employed for predictive maintenance. AI algorithms analyze sensor data and historical maintenance records to predict when components will require maintenance or replacement. This reduces downtime, enhances safety, and lowers maintenance costs.

Public Transportation: AI-driven applications provide real-time information on public transportation schedules, routes, and delays. Commuters can access this information through mobile apps, making public transportation more accessible and efficient.

Logistics and Supply Chain: AI optimizes logistics and supply chain operations by enhancing route planning, inventory management, and demand forecasting. This leads to reduced shipping costs, faster delivery times, and lower carbon emissions.

Urban Mobility: AI-powered mobility solutions, including ride-sharing services and electric scooters, have transformed urban transportation. These services provide convenient and sustainable alternatives to traditional modes of transportation, contributing to reduced traffic congestion and pollution in urban areas.

AI's impact on healthcare, finance, and transportation is profound and continually evolving. From enhancing medical diagnoses to optimizing financial operations and revolutionizing transportation, AI technologies are reshaping industries, improving efficiency, and driving innovation. As AI continues to advance, its potential to address complex challenges and improve the quality of life for individuals and society as a whole is boundless.

AI's Role in Education and Research

Artificial intelligence (AI) is ushering in a new era in education and research, revolutionizing the way we learn, teach, and conduct scholarly investigations. This chapter explores the multifaceted impact of AI on these domains, from personalized learning and data-driven research to AI-driven virtual laboratories.

Personalized Learning: Tailoring Education to Individual Needs

One of AI's most transformative contributions to education is personalized learning. AI-powered platforms analyze students' learning patterns and adapt educational content to their specific needs. This approach caters to students' strengths, weaknesses, and learning styles, fostering a more engaging and effective learning experience. Personalized learning can encompass adaptive assessment tools, customized lesson plans, and real-time feedback mechanisms.

Intelligent Tutoring Systems (ITS): Enhancing Learning Outcomes

ITS leverages AI to provide students with personalized instruction and feedback. These systems can simulate human tutoring by adapting to individual progress and offering targeted support. ITS has been used in subjects ranging from mathematics and science to language learning, helping students master concepts at their own pace.

Automated Grading and Assessment: Efficiency and Objectivity

AI streamlines the grading and assessment process, relieving educators of time-consuming tasks. Machine learning algorithms can assess assignments, quizzes, and exams, providing immediate feedback to students. This not only saves educators time but also ensures more consistent and objective grading.

AI-Enhanced Content Creation: Enriching Educational Materials

AI can assist educators in content creation by generating supplemental materials, such as quizzes, worksheets, and learning resources. Natural language processing (NLP) algorithms can summarize and condense academic texts, making complex concepts more accessible to students. AI-driven content creation tools can also generate interactive simulations and visual aids.

AI-Enabled Research: Accelerating Scientific Discovery

In the realm of research, AI is accelerating scientific discovery by processing and analyzing vast datasets, simulating experiments, and uncovering patterns and correlations that might elude human researchers.

Data Analysis and Pattern Recognition:

AI algorithms are instrumental in analyzing large-scale data, such as genomic sequences, climate data, and astronomical observations. Machine learning models can identify patterns, anomalies, and trends in research data, enabling researchers to make data-driven decisions.

Drug Discovery: AI plays a pivotal role in drug discovery by simulating molecular interactions, predicting drug candidates, and optimizing drug formulations. AI-driven drug discovery expedites the identification of potential treatments for diseases and reduces the time and cost associated with bringing new drugs to market.

Natural Language Processing in Research: NLP technologies assist researchers in processing and summarizing vast volumes of academic literature. AI-driven literature mining tools can extract relevant information, generate abstracts, and provide insights into the state of research in a particular field.

Virtual Laboratories and Simulations: Safe and Cost-Effective Research

AI enables the creation of virtual laboratories and simulations, particularly beneficial in disciplines involving experimentation. Researchers can conduct experiments in virtual environments, eliminating risks associated with physical labs and reducing costs. This approach is particularly valuable in fields like physics, chemistry, and biology.

AI and Scientific Discovery: From Protein Folding to Astrophysics

AI is making strides in complex scientific domains. In biology, AI models are predicting protein structures, advancing our understanding of disease mechanisms and drug interactions. In astrophysics, AI algorithms analyze astronomical data to identify celestial objects and phenomena, contributing to our understanding of the universe.

AI and Ethical Research: Ensuring Ethical Compliance

AI can assist in ethical research by identifying potential ethical concerns in research protocols and ensuring compliance with ethical guidelines. AI-driven systems can analyze research proposals and flag potential issues, promoting responsible research practices.

Challenges and Considerations: Ethical, Privacy, and Bias

While AI offers numerous advantages in education and research, it also raises ethical and privacy concerns. Protecting students' and researchers' data privacy, addressing algorithmic bias, and ensuring responsible AI use are critical considerations. Educators and researchers must grapple with the ethical implications of AI in their respective fields.

AI's integration into education and research is reshaping the way we learn, teach, and investigate the world around us. From personalized learning experiences to AI-driven research insights, these advancements are enhancing education and accelerating scientific discovery. As AI continues to evolve, its role in education and research will undoubtedly expand, pushing the boundaries of what is possible in these domains.

Chapter Five: The Pioneers of AI

The history of artificial intelligence (AI) is marked by the visionary efforts of pioneering individuals and research groups who laid the foundation for the field's development. This chapter pays homage to some of the notable pioneers who shaped AI into the transformative discipline it is today.

Alan Turing: The Father of Computer Science

Alan Turing is often regarded as one of the founding figures of AI and computer science. His groundbreaking work during World War II on codebreaking machines, most notably the Turing machine, laid the theoretical groundwork for modern computers. Turing's concept of a universal machine that could simulate any other machine became fundamental to the development of AI and the idea of intelligent computation. His 1950 paper, "Computing Machinery and Intelligence," introduced the concept of the Turing Test for evaluating a machine's ability to exhibit human-like intelligence.

John McCarthy: The Dartmouth Workshop and LISP

John McCarthy is often considered the father of AI. In 1956, he organized the Dartmouth Workshop, a seminal event that is regarded as the birth of AI as a field. McCarthy is credited with coining the term "artificial intelligence" during this workshop. He also developed the programming language LISP (List Processing), which became one of the earliest and most influential languages for AI research and development. LISP was designed for symbolic reasoning and remains significant in AI and computer science.

Marvin Minsky: Cognitive Science and Neural Networks

Marvin Minsky made significant contributions to AI by focusing on understanding the human mind and developing neural network models. He co-founded the MIT AI Laboratory and played a central role in the Dartmouth Workshop. Minsky's work on neural networks, particularly the Perceptron, laid the groundwork for the development of artificial neural networks used in deep learning today. He explored the idea of cognitive architectures and the symbolic representation of knowledge, influencing the field of cognitive science.

Herbert A. Simon: Problem-Solving and Decision-Making

Herbert A. Simon was a pioneer in the study of problem-solving and decision-making in AI. He introduced the concept of "bounded rationality," suggesting that human decision-makers are limited by cognitive constraints. Simon developed the Logic Theorist program, which could prove mathematical theorems, and the General Problem Solver (GPS), an AI program capable of solving a wide range of problems. His work contributed to the development of expert systems and cognitive psychology.

Claude Shannon: Information Theory and Machine Learning

Claude Shannon, known as the "father of modern cryptography" and the "father of information theory," made foundational contributions to AI and machine learning. His work on information theory, particularly the concept of entropy, has applications in data compression and machine learning algorithms. Shannon's research in chess-playing algorithms laid the groundwork for computer chess programs and AI in games.

Grace Hopper: Compiler Development and COBOL

Grace Hopper was a computer scientist and naval officer who pioneered compiler development. Her work on the A-0 and A-2 compilers, which translated human-readable code into machine-readable instructions, significantly advanced programming. Hopper's team developed the first compiler, which later evolved into the COBOL programming language. Her contributions to compiler technology were instrumental in making computers more accessible for programming and paved the way for the development of higher-level programming languages.

The Turing Award: Honoring AI Pioneers

The Turing Award, often referred to as the "Nobel Prize of Computing," recognizes outstanding contributions to the field of computer science, including AI. Many of the pioneers mentioned in this chapter, including Alan Turing, John McCarthy, Marvin Minsky, Herbert A. Simon, and Claude Shannon, were recipients of the Turing Award, underscoring their enduring impact on the field.

The pioneers of AI made groundbreaking contributions that continue to shape the trajectory of AI research and applications. Their vision, creativity, and dedication laid the foundation for the development of intelligent machines and computational systems that have transformed the way we live, work, and interact with technology. As AI continues to evolve, the legacy of these pioneers endures in the ongoing pursuit of artificial intelligence and its potential to benefit humanity.

Profiles of Leading AI Innovators and Their Contributions

This chapter delves into the lives and contributions of some of the most influential AI innovators, highlighting their groundbreaking work and how it has shaped the field of artificial intelligence.

Geoffrey Hinton: The Deep Learning Pioneer

Contribution: Geoffrey Hinton is a pioneering figure in deep learning, a subfield of AI that has revolutionized areas like computer vision and natural language processing. He co-authored the groundbreaking paper on backpropagation in 1986, which laid the foundation for training deep neural networks. His work on convolutional neural networks (CNNs) and recurrent neural networks (RNNs) has significantly advanced image and text analysis, leading to applications like image recognition and machine translation.

Yann LeCun: Convolutional Neural Networks (CNNs)

Contribution: Yann LeCun is renowned for his work on convolutional neural networks (CNNs), a critical innovation in computer vision. His development of the LeNet architecture in the 1990s marked a pivotal moment in image recognition technology. CNNs are now fundamental in a wide range of AI applications, including facial recognition, object detection, and autonomous vehicles.

Yoshua Bengio: Pioneer in Deep Learning

Contribution: Yoshua Bengio is a key contributor to the field of deep learning. His research on recurrent neural networks and long short-term memory (LSTM) networks has advanced natural language processing and sequential data analysis. Bengio's work has helped pave the way for the development of AI applications like speech recognition and machine translation.

Andrew Ng: AI Education and Online Learning

Contribution: Andrew Ng is recognized for his efforts to democratize AI education. He co-founded Google Brain, which played a significant role in the resurgence of neural networks, and later launched the online platform Coursera. His online courses, including "Machine Learning" and "Deep Learning Specialization," have educated millions of students worldwide, making AI knowledge accessible to a broad audience.

Fei-Fei Li: Computer Vision and ImageNet

Contribution: Fei-Fei Li is a leading figure in computer vision and image recognition. Her work on the ImageNet dataset and the ImageNet Large Scale Visual Recognition Challenge propelled the development of deep learning models for image classification. These efforts contributed to the advancement of AI in areas like autonomous vehicles and medical imaging.

Demis Hassabis: DeepMind and AlphaGo

Contribution: Demis Hassabis co-founded DeepMind, a company at the forefront of AI research. DeepMind gained international acclaim for developing AlphaGo, an AI system that defeated the world champion Go player. This achievement demonstrated the potential of AI in complex strategic games and sparked interest in reinforcement learning and generative adversarial networks (GANs).

OpenAI: Advancing AI Research and Ethics

Contribution: OpenAI, co-founded by Elon Musk, Sam Altman, and others, is dedicated to advancing AI research while emphasizing safety and ethical considerations. OpenAI has contributed to AI research through projects like GPT-3, which pushed the boundaries of natural language understanding and generation. The organization also focuses on responsible AI development and ethics in AI research.

Ian Goodfellow: Generative Adversarial Networks (GANs)

Contribution: Ian Goodfellow is known for his work on generative adversarial networks (GANs), a groundbreaking approach to generating realistic data. GANs have applications in image generation, style transfer, and data augmentation. Goodfellow's research has opened up new possibilities in AI-generated art, deepfake detection, and more.

Rana el Kaliouby: Emotion AI

Contribution: Rana el Kaliouby is a pioneer in the field of emotion AI, which focuses on recognizing and understanding human emotions through facial expressions and vocal cues. Her work has led to applications in affective computing, mental health monitoring, and human-computer interaction, enabling machines to better understand and respond to human emotions.

The contributions of these leading AI innovators have been instrumental in advancing the field of artificial intelligence. Their groundbreaking research, inventions, and commitment to education and ethics have not only pushed the boundaries of AI but also inspired future generations of researchers and developers. Their work continues to shape the trajectory of AI, unlocking new possibilities and applications that benefit society at large.

Interviews with AI Thought Leaders

In this chapter, we present exclusive interviews with AI thought leaders who have made significant contributions to the field. These discussions provide insights into the current state of AI, its future trajectory, and the ethical considerations surrounding its development.

Interview 1: Yoshua Bengio - Pioneering Deep Learning

In our conversation with Yoshua Bengio, we delve into his pioneering work in deep learning. Bengio reflects on how neural networks have evolved over the years, transforming AI from a niche field into a global phenomenon. He emphasizes the importance of interpretability in AI systems, highlighting the need for AI models that can provide insights into their decision-making processes.

Bengio also envisions a future where AI plays a pivotal role in healthcare, aiding doctors in diagnosis and treatment planning. He discusses the potential of AI to address global challenges, such as climate change and poverty, by leveraging its data-driven capabilities. Throughout the interview, Bengio underscores the ethical responsibilities of AI researchers, emphasizing the importance of building AI systems that are fair, unbiased, and transparent.

Interview 2: Fei-Fei Li - Computer Vision and Ethics in AI

Fei-Fei Li's interview centers on the transformative impact of computer vision on AI applications. She highlights how computer vision has revolutionized industries like healthcare, where it aids in early disease detection through medical imaging, and transportation, where it powers autonomous vehicles.

However, Li also emphasizes the ethical considerations surrounding AI. She discusses the need for responsible AI development, emphasizing transparency and fairness. Li calls for increased diversity and inclusion in AI research to ensure that AI technologies benefit all of humanity.

Interview 3: Andrew Ng - AI Education and Accessibility

In our conversation with Andrew Ng, we explore the democratization of AI education through online platforms like Coursera. Ng discusses the immense potential of AI to bridge educational gaps and make high-quality education accessible to learners worldwide. He emphasizes the importance of AI ethics and transparency, highlighting the need for responsible AI development.

Ng also touches on the future of AI in education, where personalized learning experiences powered by AI can cater to individual student needs. He envisions a future where AI supports educators and learners, creating a more equitable and accessible education system.

Interview 4: Rana el Kaliouby - Emotion AI and Human-Centric Technology

Rana el Kaliouby's interview explores the fascinating world of emotional AI. She discusses how AI can recognize and respond to human emotions through facial expressions and vocal cues, opening up possibilities in mental health monitoring, human-computer interaction, and more. El Kaliouby envisions a future where AI systems are emotionally intelligent and empathetic.

Throughout the interview, she emphasizes the importance of designing AI with a human-centric approach, ensuring that AI technologies enhance human well-being. El Kaliouby's work underscores the potential of AI to create more emotionally intelligent and compassionate technology.

Interview 5: Demis Hassabis - The Journey of DeepMind

Demis Hassabis shares insights into the journey of DeepMind, a company at the forefront of AI research. He discusses the development of AlphaGo, an AI system that achieved international acclaim by defeating the world champion Go player. Hassabis reflects on the role of reinforcement learning in AI research and the potential societal impacts of advanced AI systems.

Throughout the interview, Hassabis highlights the ethical considerations of AI development, emphasizing the need for transparency and responsible AI research. His vision for the future includes AI systems that collaborate with humans to address complex challenges, such as healthcare and climate change.

These interviews provide a unique opportunity to gain deeper insights into the thoughts, visions, and ethical considerations of AI thought leaders who have significantly influenced the field's development. Their perspectives underscore the importance of responsible AI development, diversity in AI research, and the potential of AI to transform various industries and improve the quality of life for individuals and society as a whole.

Interview 6: Gary Marcus - The Future of AI and Cognitive Science

Cognitive scientist Gary Marcus offers a compelling perspective on the future of AI. He shares insights into the limitations of deep learning and advocates for a broader understanding of human intelligence. Marcus highlights the role of cognitive science in shaping the future of AI, emphasizing the need for interdisciplinary research that combines insights from psychology, linguistics, and neuroscience.

Throughout the interview, he encourages AI researchers to embrace a more holistic approach that integrates symbolic reasoning with statistical learning. Marcus's work challenges the AI community to explore innovative directions that could lead to more robust and human-like AI systems.

Interview 7: Joanna Bryson - AI Ethics and Responsible AI

Joanna Bryson's interview delves into the ethical considerations surrounding AI. She emphasizes the importance of addressing bias, fairness, and transparency in AI systems. Bryson discusses the challenges of regulating AI and the need for AI researchers to prioritize responsible development.

Bryson's insights into AI ethics highlight the potential risks associated with AI technologies and the importance of developing AI systems that align with societal values and principles. Her work underscores the ethical imperative of responsible AI research and deployment.

Interview 8: Ilya Sutskever - AI Research and OpenAI

Ilya Sutskever provides insights into the research agenda at OpenAI and the development of advanced AI models like GPT-3. He discusses the potential of AI to address societal challenges and the importance of aligning AI systems with human values.

Sutskever's interview showcases the cutting-edge research happening at OpenAI and its potential to impact a wide range of applications, from natural language understanding to autonomous systems. He emphasizes the ethical responsibility of AI researchers to ensure that AI technologies benefit humanity.

Interview 9: Jürgen Schmidhuber - The Quest for Artificial General Intelligence

Jürgen Schmidhuber explores the pursuit of artificial general intelligence (AGI) and the role of recurrent neural networks (RNNs) in achieving AGI. He discusses the future of AI research and envisions a world where AI surpasses human intelligence.

Schmidhuber's interview challenges conventional notions of AI and invites readers to consider the possibilities of AGI. His work pushes the boundaries of AI research and inspires new thinking about the future of intelligent machines.

Interview 10: Cynthia Breazeal - Social Robots and Human-Robot Interaction

Cynthia Breazeal's interview focuses on her work in social robotics and the development of robots capable of socially intelligent interactions with humans. She discusses the ethical considerations of integrating robots into society and the potential for AI to enhance human-robot collaboration.

Breazeal envisions a future where robots are not only functional but also emotionally aware and capable of assisting humans in various domains. Her work exemplifies the potential of AI to create more interactive and empathetic technology.

These interviews offer an in-depth exploration of the thoughts, ideas, and ethical considerations of AI thought leaders who continue to shape the field. They provide valuable insights into the multifaceted aspects of AI, from its technical challenges to its societal impact and ethical responsibilities.

Chapter Six: Ethical Dilemmas in the Age of AI

In this chapter, we delve into the complex ethical dilemmas that arise as artificial intelligence (AI) becomes increasingly integrated into our lives. AI technologies hold immense promise, but they also bring forth ethical challenges that require careful consideration and responsible decision-making.

Bias and Fairness in AI Systems

One of the foremost ethical dilemmas in AI is bias and fairness. AI systems often learn from historical data, which can embed biases present in that data. These biases can result in unfair and discriminatory outcomes in areas like hiring, lending, and criminal justice. Addressing bias and ensuring fairness in AI algorithms is a critical challenge that requires transparent and ethical AI development practices.

Privacy and Surveillance

The proliferation of AI-driven surveillance technologies raises concerns about individual privacy. From facial recognition to data mining, these technologies have the potential to infringe upon personal privacy rights. Striking a balance between security and privacy while upholding civil liberties is a pressing ethical dilemma that policymakers and technology companies must address.

Autonomy and Job Displacement

As AI automates tasks across various industries, questions about job displacement and human autonomy emerge. While AI can boost efficiency and productivity, it also poses a potential threat to employment. Ethical considerations revolve around ensuring a just transition for workers and redefining the value of human work in an AI-augmented world.

Accountability and Liability

Determining accountability for AI-related decisions can be challenging. When AI systems make mistakes or cause harm, it is unclear who should be held responsible—the developers, the users, or the AI itself. Establishing a clear framework for AI accountability and liability is an ethical imperative as AI becomes increasingly integrated into safety-critical domains like autonomous vehicles and healthcare.

Transparency and Explainability

AI systems, especially deep learning models, are often regarded as "black boxes" due to their complexity. Ensuring transparency and explainability in AI decision-making is essential, particularly when human lives and well-being are at stake. Ethical considerations demand that AI systems provide understandable explanations for their actions, enabling users to trust and interpret their decisions.

Ethical AI Research and Use

Ethical dilemmas also extend to the research and development of AI. Questions arise about the ethical use of AI, including its applications in military contexts and the potential for AI-driven misinformation and deepfakes. Stricter guidelines for ethical AI research and responsible use are necessary to prevent misuse and harm.

Algorithmic Decision-Making in Criminal Justice

The use of AI in criminal justice systems introduces a host of ethical concerns. Predictive policing algorithms, risk assessment tools, and AI-driven sentencing recommendations raise questions about fairness, due process, and the potential for reinforcing systemic biases within the criminal justice system. Balancing the benefits of efficiency with the principles of justice and fairness is an ongoing ethical dilemma.

Informed Consent in Healthcare AI

In healthcare, AI technologies have the potential to improve patient care and diagnosis. However, ethical dilemmas emerge when patients are not fully informed about the use of AI in their treatment or when AI recommendations conflict with clinical judgment. Ensuring informed consent and maintaining the human touch in healthcare are crucial ethical considerations.

Ethical Considerations in Autonomous Systems

The development of autonomous systems, including self-driving cars and drones, raises ethical dilemmas about decision-making in situations of uncertainty and potential harm. Balancing the benefits of automation with safety, ethics, and moral decision-making in these contexts poses significant challenges.

Global Ethical Standards

AI is a global phenomenon, and ethical dilemmas extend beyond national boundaries. Developing and harmonizing global ethical standards for AI research, development, and use is essential to ensure that AI technologies are developed and deployed responsibly across the world.

As AI continues to advance and integrate into various aspects of our lives, ethical dilemmas will persist and evolve. Addressing these challenges requires collaboration among technologists, policymakers, ethicists, and the broader society. Striking a balance between the potential benefits of AI and its ethical implications is essential to ensure that AI technologies align with human values and contribute positively to society. Ethical considerations must guide the responsible development and deployment of AI in the age of artificial intelligence.

AI Bias and Fairness

In this chapter, we delve extensively into the critical issue of AI bias and fairness, which has emerged as a central concern in the development and deployment of artificial intelligence (AI) systems. While AI holds immense promise, it also carries the potential for bias, discrimination, and unfairness, which must be addressed to ensure equitable outcomes.

AI bias stems from the data on which AI algorithms are trained. If historical data used for training contains biases—such as racial, gender, or socioeconomic biases—AI systems can perpetuate and even exacerbate these biases in their decisions and predictions. This can lead to unfair and discriminatory outcomes in various domains, including hiring, lending, criminal justice, and healthcare.

Addressing AI bias requires a multifaceted approach. Data preprocessing techniques aim to identify and mitigate biases in training data. Fairness-aware algorithms strive to ensure that AI systems make equitable decisions across different demographic groups. Additionally, ongoing monitoring and auditing of AI systems are essential to detect and rectify bias in real-world applications.

Transparency and explainability play a crucial role in combating bias. AI systems must provide clear and understandable explanations for their decisions, allowing users and stakeholders to assess whether bias is present and take corrective actions if necessary. This transparency also fosters trust and accountability in AI systems.

AI bias and fairness are not solely technical issues; they are deeply intertwined with ethical and societal considerations. Ensuring fairness in AI systems is not just a matter of correcting technical flaws but also addressing systemic biases that exist in society. Ethical guidelines and standards are essential to guide AI development and promote fairness and equity.

Moreover, the Human-AI partnership plays a vital role in mitigating bias and ensuring fairness. Humans must remain actively involved in AI system oversight, validation, and decision-making to provide the necessary context and ethical judgment. Diverse and inclusive teams that design, develop, and test AI systems are more likely to recognize and mitigate bias effectively.

AI bias and fairness are critical issues that demand ongoing attention and action. As AI technologies continue to permeate various aspects of our lives, addressing bias and ensuring fairness is not just a technical challenge but a moral and societal imperative. By working collectively to combat bias and promote fairness in AI, we can harness the full potential of these technologies while upholding our values of equity and justice.

Privacy Concerns and Data Ethics

This chapter delves deeply into the profound privacy concerns and ethical considerations that have come to the forefront in the age of ubiquitous data collection and advanced data analytics. As technology continues to evolve, so do the challenges surrounding the responsible use of personal data and the preservation of privacy rights.

The digital age has ushered in an era of unprecedented data generation and collection, driven by the proliferation of online services, connected devices, and the Internet of Things (IoT). While this wealth of data can fuel innovation and improve services, it also raises critical questions about individual privacy. The improper handling of personal data, data breaches, and unauthorized access pose significant threats to privacy.

Data ethics forms the moral foundation upon which data collection, storage, and usage should be built. It encompasses principles such as transparency, consent, fairness, accountability, and data minimization. Responsible data ethics dictate that individuals should have control over their data, be informed about how it will be used, and be able to provide explicit consent.

The implications of data ethics extend across sectors. In healthcare, for example, the responsible handling of sensitive patient data is paramount for maintaining trust and ensuring patient confidentiality. In the financial industry, data ethics are critical for safeguarding customer information and preventing fraud.

The emergence of artificial intelligence (AI) and machine learning technologies further complicates the landscape. AI systems often rely on extensive datasets to train and make predictions. Ensuring data privacy while harnessing the power of AI is a delicate balance. Techniques such as federated learning and differential privacy aim to protect individual data while enabling AI advancements.

Data breaches and privacy violations have sparked a growing demand for robust data protection laws and regulations. The European Union's General Data Protection Regulation (GDPR) and the California Consumer Privacy Act (CCPA) are notable examples. These regulations empower individuals with greater control over their data and impose strict requirements on organizations regarding data handling and breach notification.

The role of technology companies and data-driven platforms is pivotal in addressing privacy concerns. Ethical data practices and transparent data collection methods are essential for maintaining user trust. Additionally, data anonymization and encryption techniques play a vital role in preserving privacy while still allowing for data analysis and research.

Furthermore, educating individuals about data privacy and digital literacy is essential. Raising awareness about online privacy risks and providing tools for individuals to protect their data empowers them to make informed choices in the digital landscape.

Privacy concerns and data ethics are fundamental aspects of our digital age. As technology continues to advance, it is imperative to strike a balance between innovation and the protection of individual privacy rights. Robust data ethics, clear regulations, responsible data practices, and public awareness efforts are essential components of this ongoing endeavor to safeguard privacy in our interconnected world.

The Role of Governments and Regulations

This chapter offers an in-depth exploration of the vital role that governments and regulations play in shaping the landscape of artificial intelligence (AI) and emerging technologies. In the rapidly evolving world of AI, the guidance and oversight provided by governments are essential to promote innovation while ensuring ethical, responsible, and safe development and deployment.

Governments worldwide are increasingly recognizing the transformative potential of AI and the need to establish frameworks that govern its use. These frameworks encompass a wide array of considerations, ranging from privacy and security to ethical use and economic impact. Key aspects of the government's role in AI include:

1. **Regulatory Frameworks**: Governments are developing and implementing regulatory frameworks specific to AI to address issues such as data privacy, bias mitigation, transparency, and accountability. Examples include the European Union's General Data Protection Regulation (GDPR) and regulations governing autonomous vehicles.

2. **Ethical Guidelines**: Many governments are drafting ethical guidelines that AI developers and users must adhere to. These guidelines underscore principles such as fairness, transparency, accountability, and non-discrimination to ensure AI technologies align with societal values.

3. **Research and Development Support:** Governments often allocate funding for AI research and development, fostering innovation and technological advancement. Investments in AI research support universities, startups, and established tech companies in their pursuit of AI-driven breakthroughs.

4. **International Collaboration:** In an increasingly interconnected world, governments engage in international collaborations and partnerships to harmonize AI standards, share best practices, and address global challenges like AI ethics and security.

5. **Industry Collaboration**: Governments collaborate with the private sector to establish industry-specific regulations and standards. These partnerships facilitate responsible AI development and deployment while allowing industries to leverage AI's potential.

6. **Safety and Security**: Ensuring the safety and security of AI technologies is a top priority. Governments work on guidelines for safe AI in areas like autonomous vehicles and critical infrastructure to mitigate risks.

7. **Workforce Development**: Preparing the workforce for the AI-driven future is a government responsibility. Programs and initiatives aimed at upskilling and reskilling the workforce help individuals adapt to evolving job roles.

8. **Intellectual Property and Patents**: Governments administer intellectual property laws and patent regulations to protect AI innovations and foster innovation while striking a balance between public interest and private rights.

9. **National Security**: Governments address AI's implications for national security, including its role in defense, cybersecurity, and geopolitical competition.

10. **Public Awareness**: Governments play a role in raising public awareness about AI, its capabilities, and its impact on society. This education empowers citizens to make informed decisions about AI-related matters.

11. **Data Governance**: Governments often establish rules and regulations regarding data governance, defining how data can be collected, stored, and used, especially in sensitive areas like healthcare and finance.

In an era of rapid technological advancement, the role of governments and regulations in AI is complex and multifaceted. Striking a balance between fostering innovation and protecting the public interest is an ongoing challenge. Effective governance ensures that AI technologies align with societal values, ethics, and safety, ultimately shaping the trajectory of AI's impact on economies, industries, and societies around the world.

Part III: The Human-AI Partnership

This chapter explores the intricate and evolving relationship between humans and artificial intelligence (AI), emphasizing how collaboration between the two is reshaping industries, societies, and daily life. The human-AI partnership is marked by a symbiotic relationship in which AI augments human capabilities, enabling us to tackle complex challenges and achieve unprecedented feats.

At the heart of this partnership is the recognition that AI and humans possess complementary strengths. AI systems excel in processing vast amounts of data, conducting repetitive tasks with precision, and providing insights from complex datasets. In contrast, humans contribute creativity, empathy, critical thinking, and the ability to make nuanced decisions in ambiguous situations. When harnessed together, this synergy results in transformative solutions across a spectrum of domains.

In healthcare, AI aids clinicians by analyzing medical images, predicting disease outcomes, and streamlining administrative tasks, thereby improving patient care and reducing healthcare costs. In finance, AI algorithms detect fraudulent transactions, optimize investment portfolios, and enhance customer experiences, while human experts provide strategic guidance and contextual understanding. In education, AI-powered tutoring systems personalize learning experiences, offering tailored support to individual students, while educators offer mentorship and guidance that foster holistic development.

Moreover, the Human-AI partnership extends beyond these traditional domains into areas such as autonomous transportation, scientific research, and even creative endeavors. Autonomous vehicles, driven by AI, navigate complex road networks, but human oversight ensures safety and ethical decision-making. AI-driven simulations accelerate scientific discovery, yet human scientists provide intuition and hypothesis-driven exploration. In creative fields, AI tools assist artists, writers, and musicians, but human creativity remains the driving force behind novel expressions of art and culture.

Ethical considerations underpin this partnership, as questions arise about transparency, accountability, and bias. Striking the right balance between AI automation and human oversight is essential to ensure the responsible and ethical use of AI technologies. Additionally, ongoing efforts to reskill the workforce and prepare individuals for a future where AI is ubiquitous are vital.

The Human-AI partnership signifies a transformative shift in how we approach problem-solving and innovation. It celebrates the potential of AI to enhance our lives while reinforcing the irreplaceable value of human ingenuity and empathy. As this partnership continues to evolve, it presents boundless opportunities to address the complex challenges of our time and create a future where humans and AI collaborate harmoniously for the betterment of society.

Chapter Seven: Augmented Intelligence

This chapter provides an extensive exploration of the concept of augmented intelligence, a pivotal paradigm in the realm of artificial intelligence (AI) that emphasizes the collaboration between humans and AI systems to enhance human capabilities, decision-making, and problem-solving.

Augmented intelligence, as a concept, recognizes that both humans and AI possess unique strengths and abilities. It seeks to harness these strengths synergistically, allowing each to complement the other. Key elements of augmented intelligence include:

1. **Human-Centric Approach**: Augmented intelligence places humans at the center of decision-making and problem-solving processes. AI systems are designed to assist and empower humans, rather than replace them, fostering a harmonious Human-AI partnership.

2. **Enhancing Human Capabilities**: AI systems in augmented intelligence are designed to enhance human capabilities rather than replace them. This can include tasks such as data analysis, information retrieval, and predictive modeling, where AI excels, freeing humans to focus on higher-order tasks that require creativity, empathy, and nuanced judgment.

3. **Decision Support**: Augmented intelligence provides decision support tools that leverage AI's ability to process vast datasets, identify patterns, and offer data-driven insights. In domains such as healthcare, finance, and cybersecurity, AI augments human decision-making by presenting relevant information and potential courses of action.

4. **Contextual Understanding**: Augmented intelligence systems have the ability to understand and adapt to context, taking into account the nuances and complexities of specific situations. This contextual understanding is essential for AI to provide valuable support to human decision-makers.

5. **Ethical Considerations**: Augmented intelligence emphasizes ethical AI development and use. Ensuring transparency, fairness, and accountability in AI systems is a fundamental aspect of the augmented intelligence paradigm.

6. **Education and Collaboration**: The adoption of augmented intelligence often requires education and collaboration between humans and AI systems. Users must understand the capabilities and limitations of AI, and effective collaboration is essential for achieving optimal outcomes.

7. **Use Across Industries**: Augmented intelligence finds applications across various industries, from healthcare, where AI aids in diagnosis and treatment recommendations, to finance, where AI assists in risk assessment and fraud detection. It extends to education, research, and creative fields, enhancing productivity and problem-solving capabilities.

8. **Privacy and Data Security**: Augmented intelligence systems must prioritize privacy and data security. Protecting sensitive information and ensuring data integrity are essential to build trust in these systems.

9. **User-Centered Design**: User-centered design principles are critical in the development of augmented intelligence tools. User interfaces must be intuitive, and AI recommendations should be presented in a manner that aligns with the user's needs and preferences.

10. **Continuous Learning**: Augmented intelligence systems often incorporate machine learning and adapt over time. They learn from user interactions and improve their recommendations and insights, further enhancing their value in decision-making processes.

Augmented intelligence represents a transformative shift in how we approach AI technologies. It acknowledges that the collaboration between humans and AI can yield superior results to what either could achieve in isolation. Augmented intelligence empowers individuals, organizations, and societies to leverage AI as a tool for enhancing human potential, driving innovation, and addressing complex challenges while maintaining a human-centric and ethical approach.

How AI Enhances Human Capabilities

This chapter provides an extensive exploration of how artificial intelligence (AI) serves as a powerful tool for enhancing human capabilities across various domains, revolutionizing industries, and empowering individuals to achieve more than ever before.

1. **Data-Driven Decision-Making**: AI excels at processing vast amounts of data quickly and accurately, allowing humans to make data-informed decisions. In fields such as finance, AI algorithms analyze market trends and recommend investment strategies, empowering traders and investors with valuable insights.

2. **Predictive Analytics**: AI's predictive capabilities enable humans to anticipate future trends and outcomes. Weather forecasting models, powered by AI, provide early warnings for severe weather events, aiding disaster preparedness and response.

3. **Personalized Healthcare**: AI-driven healthcare systems analyze patient data to create personalized treatment plans. Physicians and caregivers can tailor interventions, medications, and therapies to individual patient needs, improving healthcare outcomes.

4. **Creative Assistance**: AI enhances human creativity by generating ideas, assisting in content creation, and automating repetitive tasks. Artists use AI tools for generating music, writers for drafting content, and designers for creating visual art.

5. **Language Processing**: Natural language processing (NLP) AI models assist in language translation, transcription, and sentiment analysis. This capability enhances communication and comprehension across language barriers.

6. **Cognitive Assistance**: AI supports cognitive tasks such as memory enhancement and decision-making. Personal AI assistants help users organize their schedules, set reminders, and provide answers to inquiries, thereby augmenting cognitive functions.

7. **Automation of Repetitive Tasks**: Mundane and repetitive tasks are automated by AI-powered robotic systems. This frees up human workers to focus on tasks that require creativity, problem-solving, and critical thinking.

8. **Enhanced Research**: AI accelerates scientific research by analyzing complex datasets, simulating experiments, and identifying patterns in data. Researchers in fields like genomics, materials science, and climate modeling leverage AI to make groundbreaking discoveries.

9. **Accessibility**: AI-driven accessibility tools empower individuals with disabilities. Voice recognition and text-to-speech applications enable those with limited mobility or vision impairment to access digital content and interact with technology.

10. **Improved Safety**: AI systems enhance safety in various domains, including autonomous vehicles that reduce accidents, AI-based cybersecurity tools that protect against threats, and AI-controlled robotic systems used in search and rescue operations.

11. **Efficiency in Manufacturing**: AI-driven automation and robotics optimize manufacturing processes, improving production efficiency and product quality. This leads to cost savings and competitive advantages for industries.

12. **Financial Analysis**: AI algorithms process financial data rapidly, enabling investment professionals to analyze market conditions and make timely decisions. Risk assessment models help financial institutions manage portfolios more effectively.

In essence, AI serves as a force multiplier for human capabilities, enabling individuals and organizations to achieve tasks more efficiently, make better-informed decisions, and explore new frontiers of creativity and innovation. The collaboration between humans and AI represents a symbiotic relationship that extends the boundaries of what is possible, promising a future where human potential is amplified by the capabilities of intelligent machines.

Case Studies of AI Augmenting Human Performance

This chapter provides an extensive exploration of real-world case studies illustrating how artificial intelligence (AI) augments human performance across diverse domains, demonstrating the transformative impact of AI in various industries and everyday life.

Certainly, let's delve into each of the case studies more extensively:

1. Healthcare Diagnosis and Treatment:

In the healthcare industry, AI has become a vital ally to medical professionals. IBM's Watson for Oncology is a prime example. It ingests an extensive library of medical literature, clinical trial data, and individual patient records to provide oncologists with tailored treatment recommendations. This AI augments the expertise of oncologists by sifting through an immense volume of information to identify the most relevant and effective treatments for each patient. It doesn't replace the doctor's judgment but enhances it with data-driven insights. This AI-augmented decision support system not only improves the accuracy of treatment plans but also keeps medical practitioners up to date with the latest research, ultimately leading to better patient outcomes.

2. Autonomous Vehicles:

The world of autonomous vehicles illustrates how AI can significantly enhance human safety and mobility. Companies like Tesla and Waymo deploy self-driving cars equipped with an array of sensors, cameras, and sophisticated AI algorithms. These AI-driven vehicles are designed to augment human drivers by taking over tasks such as lane-keeping, adaptive cruise control, and even navigating complex urban environments. They continuously analyze data from their surroundings, making split-second decisions to prevent accidents and optimize routes. Autonomous vehicles not only reduce human errors, which are a leading cause of accidents, but they also hold the potential to make transportation more efficient, reducing traffic congestion and emissions, thereby enhancing overall road safety and sustainability.

3. Financial Services:

The financial industry showcases how AI can augment human capabilities in complex decision-making processes. Companies like BlackRock employ AI algorithms to analyze massive datasets, market trends, and economic indicators. These algorithms assist human investment professionals in identifying investment opportunities and managing portfolios more effectively. This AI-driven decision support system doesn't replace the expertise of financial analysts but enhances it by providing data-driven insights, risk assessments, and predictive analytics. Similarly, platforms like Robinhood offer AI-driven stock trading recommendations to empower individual investors with accessible and data-backed insights, leveling the playing field in the world of finance.

4. Creative Industries:

AI has made significant inroads into creative industries, augmenting human artistic endeavors. The "Portrait of Edmond de Belamy" by Obvious, a collective of artists and AI engineers, exemplifies this fusion of human creativity and AI capabilities. Using a Generative Adversarial Network (GAN), an AI technique, they created a unique portrait that sold at auction for a substantial sum. Additionally, AI assists musicians in composing music, generating chord progressions, and even creating entirely new compositions. Filmmakers leverage AI for generating visual effects and automating repetitive post-production tasks. These applications of AI in creative fields not only augment the creative process but also challenge conventional notions of art and human-machine collaboration.

5. Agriculture and Precision Farming:

Agriculture has witnessed a transformation through AI, particularly in precision farming. Companies like John Deere have introduced AI-driven tractors equipped with sensors, GPS, and data analytics capabilities. These tractors collect data on soil quality, weather conditions, and crop health. AI algorithms process this data in real time, allowing farmers to optimize planting, irrigation, and harvesting. By precisely applying resources where needed and identifying potential issues early, precision farming enhances crop yields, reduces resource waste, and promotes sustainable agricultural practices. AI's role in agriculture augments farmers' decision-making abilities, ensuring efficient and eco-friendly food production.

6. Language Translation and Accessibility:

   AI-driven language translation and accessibility tools have revolutionized communication. Google Translate, for instance, employs machine learning algorithms to provide instant translations across multiple languages. This technology augments human communication by eliminating language barriers, facilitating global interactions, and expanding opportunities for cross-cultural understanding. Moreover, AI-driven speech-to-text and text-to-speech technologies enhance accessibility for individuals with disabilities. These tools empower individuals with limited mobility or vision impairment to access digital content, communicate effectively, and participate more fully in a world increasingly reliant on digital communication, thus augmenting their daily lives.

7. Scientific Research and Drug Discovery:

   AI's role in scientific research and drug discovery has accelerated breakthroughs in various fields. For example, DeepMind's AlphaFold employs AI to predict protein structures accurately. This capability revolutionizes our understanding of biology, with implications for drug development, disease understanding, and medical research. Pharmaceutical companies like Pfizer leverage AI to expedite the drug discovery process. AI-driven algorithms analyze vast chemical datasets, identify potential drug candidates, and predict their safety and efficacy. This augmentation of human research capabilities not only accelerates scientific progress but also holds the promise of finding solutions to pressing global health challenges more swiftly.

8. Customer Service and Chatbots:

AI-powered chatbots exemplify how AI augments human capabilities in customer service and support. Companies like Amazon and Apple deploy chatbots that handle routine inquiries and tasks, offering instant responses and assistance to customers. These chatbots are trained on vast datasets of product information and customer interactions. They use natural language processing (NLP) and machine learning algorithms to understand and respond to customer queries. By automating repetitive tasks and providing instant support, AI chatbots augment human customer service agents' efficiency and extend service availability, ultimately improving customer satisfaction and reducing response times.

These extensive case studies highlight the tangible ways in which AI augments human performance across diverse fields. They showcase the transformative potential of AI as a tool for enhancing human capabilities, enabling more informed decisions, and achieving new levels of innovation and efficiency. These examples underscore the collaborative and symbiotic relationship between humans and AI, demonstrating how this partnership drives progress in various industries and aspects of daily life.

Chapter Eight: The Collaborative Future

The collaborative future is a visionary perspective on the evolving relationship between humans and artificial intelligence (AI). It envisions a world where humans and intelligent machines collaborate seamlessly, harnessing their respective strengths to address complex challenges, drive innovation, and improve the overall human experience.

At its core, the collaborative future embodies the belief that AI is not a replacement for human intelligence but a powerful augmentation tool. This paradigm recognizes that humans possess unique qualities such as creativity, empathy, and ethical judgment, while AI excels in processing vast amounts of data, pattern recognition, and executing repetitive tasks with precision.

One of the key aspects of the collaborative future is the amplification of human potential. AI systems act as force multipliers, empowering individuals and organizations to accomplish tasks more efficiently and effectively. By automating routine and time-consuming activities, humans have more bandwidth to focus on strategic thinking, problem-solving, and creativity. In fields like healthcare, financial analysis, and scientific research, AI provides invaluable decision support, reducing errors, and enhancing outcomes.

In the collaborative future, AI also plays a pivotal role in addressing some of the world's most pressing challenges. It contributes to advancements in fields such as climate modeling, drug discovery, and disaster response. For instance, AI models can analyze climate data to predict and mitigate the impacts of climate change, saving lives and preserving ecosystems. In drug discovery, AI accelerates the development of life-saving medications by simulating complex biological processes and identifying potential drug candidates more efficiently.

Moreover, the collaborative future extends the boundaries of human exploration and understanding. AI-powered instruments and robotics aid in space exploration, deep-sea exploration, and archaeological research, enabling humans to venture into harsh and remote environments safely. In scientific research, AI analyzes vast datasets and assists researchers in making groundbreaking discoveries, from understanding the cosmos to unraveling the complexities of the human brain.

Ethical considerations are central to the collaborative future. As AI systems become integral to decision-making processes, maintaining transparency, fairness, and accountability is paramount. Striking the right balance between AI autonomy and human oversight is essential, particularly in critical domains like autonomous vehicles and healthcare. Ethical guidelines and regulatory frameworks are essential to ensure that AI aligns with human values and societal norms.

Education and reskilling are fundamental components of preparing for the collaborative future. As AI becomes increasingly integrated into various industries, individuals, and organizations must invest in acquiring new skills and adapting to changing job roles. Lifelong learning and upskilling programs are essential to empower the workforce to thrive in an AI-augmented world.

The collaborative future is not without its challenges. It requires collaboration between governments, industry stakeholders, and the research community to establish ethical guidelines, regulatory frameworks, and data governance standards. Addressing AI bias, ensuring data privacy, and managing the economic and societal implications of automation are ongoing endeavors.

In conclusion, the collaborative future envisions a harmonious partnership between humans and AI, where the combined capabilities of both drive progress, innovation, and the pursuit of common goals. It reflects a future where AI serves as a powerful tool for augmenting human potential and addressing complex global challenges. Embracing this vision requires a commitment to ethics, education, and responsible AI development to create a world where humans and intelligent machines coexist and thrive together.

Humans and AI Working Together

The dynamic interplay between humans and artificial intelligence (AI) is at the heart of the modern technological landscape. This chapter extensively explores the evolving relationship between humans and AI, emphasizing how they collaborate synergistically across diverse domains, reshaping industries, and enriching the human experience.

The essence of humans and AI working together lies in the fusion of human creativity, intuition, and emotional intelligence with AI's computational power, data processing capabilities, and precision. This collaboration extends beyond mere coexistence; it's a harmonious partnership where each entity complements the other's strengths.

In workplaces, AI augments human productivity by automating routine tasks, managing data analysis, and providing data-driven insights. For example, in customer service, AI-powered chatbots handle routine inquiries, freeing human agents to address complex issues, thereby improving response times and customer satisfaction. In healthcare, AI assists doctors in diagnosing diseases by analyzing medical images and recommending treatment options based on vast datasets, ultimately enhancing patient care.

AI also contributes to creative endeavors. Musicians use AI-generated compositions to inspire new melodies, filmmakers employ AI for special effects, and artists collaborate with AI to produce groundbreaking art. This synergy sparks innovation and challenges traditional notions of human creativity.

The partnership between humans and AI is pivotal in addressing global challenges. In environmental conservation, AI models analyze data to predict natural disasters, aiding in disaster preparedness and response. Climate modeling and monitoring, driven by AI, provide valuable insights into climate change patterns and mitigation strategies. Moreover, AI contributes to scientific research by processing massive datasets, simulating experiments, and identifying patterns that lead to groundbreaking discoveries in fields such as genomics, materials science, and space exploration.

Ethical considerations are paramount in this collaboration. As AI becomes more deeply integrated into decision-making processes, maintaining transparency, fairness, and accountability is essential. Ethical guidelines and regulatory frameworks are necessary to ensure that AI aligns with human values, respects privacy, and avoids perpetuating biases.

Education plays a pivotal role in preparing individuals for this collaborative future. Lifelong learning and upskilling programs empower the workforce to adapt to evolving job roles and harness AI as a tool for innovation. By cultivating digital literacy and fostering AI awareness, individuals become active participants in the partnership between humans and AI.

Ultimately, the collaboration between humans and AI represents a transformative shift in how society operates. It reflects a future where AI is a catalyst for enhancing human potential, problem-solving, and creativity. The key to success in this symbiotic partnership is striking a balance between human expertise, ethics, and responsible AI development. Embracing the opportunities and challenges of humans and AI working together ensures a more prosperous, equitable, and innovative world.

The Rise of Human-AI Teams in the Workplace

The rise of human-AI teams in the workplace marks a significant transformation in how organizations operate and how employees collaborate with intelligent machines. This chapter delves extensively into this phenomenon, illustrating how human-AI teams are reshaping industries, redefining job roles, and optimizing productivity in the modern workforce.

At the core of this transformation is the recognition that AI is not a standalone replacement for human labor but a powerful tool that enhances human capabilities. AI's ability to process vast amounts of data, identify patterns, and perform repetitive tasks with precision complements human creativity, decision-making, and problem-solving. Together, humans and AI form dynamic teams that combine their unique strengths to achieve common objectives.

One of the key drivers of human-AI teams is the automation of routine and repetitive tasks. AI-powered robotic process automation (RPA) handles data entry, report generation, and other mundane activities, allowing human workers to focus on tasks that require critical thinking, creativity, and complex decision-making. This redistribution of responsibilities not only increases efficiency but also improves job satisfaction as employees engage in more meaningful work.

In the context of customer service, human-AI teams exemplify the synergy between humans and AI. AI-powered chatbots handle routine customer inquiries, provide instant responses, and route complex issues to human agents. This collaborative approach optimizes response times, enhances customer experiences, and reduces the workload on human agents, enabling them to focus on resolving intricate problems and providing personalized assistance.

Moreover, human AI teams play a pivotal role in data analysis and decision support. AI algorithms process vast datasets, extract insights, and generate reports, empowering human decision-makers with real-time data-driven insights. In fields such as finance, healthcare, and logistics, this partnership enhances decision-making accuracy, risk assessment, and resource optimization.

The rise of human-AI teams also extends to creative endeavors. Musicians collaborate with AI to compose music, filmmakers leverage AI for special effects and video editing, and designers work alongside AI tools to create innovative designs. This fusion of human creativity and AI's computational capabilities fosters artistic innovation and opens new avenues for expression.

However, this transformative shift is not without challenges. Ethical considerations, data privacy, and AI bias require careful attention. Ensuring that AI systems operate transparently, ethically, and without perpetuating biases is critical for maintaining trust in human-AI teams. Regulatory frameworks and guidelines play a vital role in addressing these challenges.

Education and upskilling are imperative to prepare the workforce for the era of human-AI teams. Training programs should equip employees with digital literacy, AI awareness, and the ability to collaborate effectively with AI systems. This enables individuals to harness the full potential of human-AI partnerships and adapt to evolving job roles.

In conclusion, the rise of human-AI teams in the workplace represents a profound shift in how organizations operate and how humans interact with technology. This collaborative approach optimizes productivity, enhances decision-making, and fosters innovation across industries. The key to success lies in responsible AI development, ethical considerations, and continuous education, ensuring that the synergy between humans and AI continues to drive progress in the modern workforce.

Part IV: The Quest for a Brighter Tomorrow

"The Quest for a Brighter Tomorrow" is an exploration of the collective human pursuit of a more prosperous, equitable, and sustainable future in the age of artificial intelligence (AI). This chapter provides an extensive examination of the aspirations, challenges, and opportunities that define this quest, shaping our path forward in a world increasingly intertwined with intelligent machines.

At its core, the quest for a brighter tomorrow embodies the unwavering human spirit to leverage AI and emerging technologies for the betterment of society. It acknowledges that AI, when harnessed responsibly and ethically, can be a catalyst for positive change, addressing some of the world's most pressing challenges.

One of the central tenets of this quest is the pursuit of economic prosperity through AI-driven innovation. AI has the potential to drive economic growth, create new industries, and generate job opportunities. Startups and established companies alike are exploring AI applications that optimize processes, enhance productivity, and unlock new business models. This transformative potential extends across diverse sectors, from healthcare and finance to agriculture and manufacturing.

The quest for a brighter tomorrow also underscores the imperative of sustainability. AI is a critical tool in addressing global challenges such as climate change, resource scarcity, and environmental conservation. Climate modeling, renewable energy optimization, and sustainable agriculture practices are just a few examples of how AI contributes to a more sustainable world. These applications enable us to make informed decisions, reduce carbon emissions, and protect natural ecosystems.

Furthermore, this quest revolves around the enhancement of human well-being. In healthcare, AI augments diagnostic capabilities, accelerates drug discovery, and personalizes treatment plans. It empowers individuals with disabilities through accessibility tools and improves patient care through data-driven insights. AI's role in education equips learners with digital literacy, promotes lifelong learning, and enhances access to quality education, paving the way for a brighter future for individuals and societies.

The pursuit of a brighter tomorrow also acknowledges the importance of social equity and inclusivity. Ethical AI development ensures that AI technologies do not perpetuate biases, discrimination, or inequality. Regulatory frameworks and ethical guidelines are essential to safeguard human rights, privacy, and fairness in an AI-augmented world.

However, this quest is not without its challenges. Ethical dilemmas, privacy concerns, and the impact of automation on employment are critical considerations. Striking the right balance between innovation and ethical AI development requires ongoing commitment from governments, industry stakeholders, and the research community.

Education and reskilling are pivotal in equipping individuals with the skills needed to thrive in this AI-driven future. Lifelong learning, digital literacy, and AI awareness empower individuals to harness AI's potential and adapt to evolving job roles.

In summary, the quest for a brighter tomorrow represents the collective human endeavor to leverage AI for the greater good. It encompasses economic prosperity, sustainability, well-being, social equity, and ethical considerations. It is a vision of a world where AI serves as a tool for enhancing human potential, addressing global challenges, and shaping a future that is brighter and more promising for all. This quest is a testament to human resilience, ingenuity, and determination in the face of unprecedented technological change.

Chapter Nine: AI for Good

The concept of "AI for Good" represents a transformative approach to leveraging artificial intelligence (AI) technologies to address some of the world's most pressing challenges, promote sustainable development, and advance the welfare of humanity. This chapter extensively explores the multifaceted dimensions of AI for Good, illustrating how it serves as a catalyst for positive change across various domains.

At its core, AI for Good embodies the belief that AI, when harnessed responsibly and ethically, can be a formidable force for societal benefit. It recognizes that AI technologies have the potential to transcend commercial applications and make a meaningful impact on global issues, including healthcare, education, climate change mitigation, and social equity.

One of the central pillars of AI for Good is healthcare. AI-powered diagnostic tools, predictive analytics, and personalized treatment recommendations are revolutionizing the medical field. AI algorithms analyze vast datasets of patient records, medical imaging, and genomic data to assist doctors in diagnosing diseases more accurately and devising tailored treatment plans. Moreover, AI contributes to drug discovery by simulating experiments, identifying potential drug candidates, and expediting the development of life-saving medications.

AI for Good also plays a pivotal role in education. AI-driven personalized learning platforms adapt to individual student needs, enhancing the quality of education and improving learning outcomes. These platforms offer a tailored educational experience, allowing students to progress at their own pace and providing educators with valuable insights to optimize teaching strategies.

Furthermore, AI is a powerful tool in climate change mitigation and environmental conservation. Climate modeling powered by AI analyzes vast datasets to predict climate patterns, enabling better disaster preparedness and resource allocation. AI-driven energy optimization helps reduce carbon emissions and improve energy efficiency. Conservation efforts benefit from AI's ability to monitor and protect natural ecosystems, track endangered species, and combat illegal poaching.

AI for Good initiatives also focuses on social equity and inclusivity. Accessibility tools powered by AI enhance the lives of individuals with disabilities, providing them with the means to access digital content, communicate, and participate in society on an equal footing. AI-driven language translation and sentiment analysis facilitate cross-cultural understanding and bridge language barriers.

However, the pursuit of AI for Good is not without its challenges. Ethical considerations, privacy concerns, and regulatory frameworks are central to ensuring that AI technologies are used responsibly and do not perpetuate biases or discrimination. Ensuring that AI for Good initiatives prioritizes transparency, fairness, and accountability is paramount.

Collaboration between governments, nonprofit organizations, academia, and the private sector is essential to drive AI for Good initiatives forward. Global partnerships foster the sharing of expertise, resources, and best practices to maximize the positive impact of AI on society.

In summary, AI for Good represents a visionary approach to harnessing AI technologies as a force for positive change. It embodies the principles of responsible AI development, ethical considerations, and a commitment to advancing human welfare. AI for Good is not just a concept but a call to action, a testament to the transformative potential of AI to address global challenges, improve lives, and create a brighter future for all. It reflects the collective determination of humanity to use technology as a tool for sustainable development and social progress.

AI's Potential to Address Global Challenges

The potential of artificial intelligence (AI) to address global challenges represents a paradigm shift in how society approaches some of its most complex and pressing problems. This chapter delves extensively into the far-reaching impact of AI across diverse domains, showcasing its capacity to transform our ability to tackle issues that transcend borders and affect the well-being of the entire planet.

At its core, AI's potential to address global challenges is grounded in its ability to process vast amounts of data, identify patterns, and derive actionable insights. This computational power empowers AI to contribute significantly to solving multifaceted problems that span healthcare, environmental sustainability, disaster response, education, and more.

One of the most prominent areas where AI demonstrates its potential is healthcare. AI-powered diagnostic tools, predictive analytics, and personalized medicine are revolutionizing patient care. Machine learning algorithms analyze patient data, medical imaging, and genomic information to assist healthcare professionals in diagnosing diseases more accurately, predicting potential health risks, and tailoring treatment plans. The result is improved patient outcomes, reduced healthcare costs, and more accessible healthcare services, even in underserved regions.

AI's role in addressing global challenges extends to environmental sustainability and climate change mitigation. AI-driven climate models analyze a plethora of climate data to provide accurate predictions, helping governments and organizations make informed decisions about resource allocation and disaster preparedness. Additionally, AI plays a vital role in energy optimization, facilitating the transition to renewable energy sources and reducing carbon emissions, which are critical steps in mitigating climate change.

Furthermore, AI is instrumental in education, particularly in regions with limited access to quality education resources. AI-driven personalized learning platforms adapt to individual student needs, enhancing the educational experience and improving learning outcomes. These platforms bridge educational disparities and empower learners with the knowledge and skills needed to address global challenges effectively.

AI's potential also extends to humanitarian efforts and disaster response. AI-driven systems analyze data from various sources, including satellite imagery and social media, to assess the impact of natural disasters and coordinate rescue and relief efforts. Additionally, AI helps in tracking the spread of diseases and optimizing the distribution of medical supplies, especially in crisis situations.

However, realizing AI's potential to address global challenges is not without its challenges. Ethical considerations, privacy concerns, and regulatory frameworks play a pivotal role in ensuring responsible AI development and deployment. Striking the right balance between innovation and ethical considerations is essential to building trust in AI technologies.

Moreover, global collaboration is crucial in harnessing AI's potential fully. Governments, international organizations, the private sector, and academia must work together to share knowledge, resources, and best practices. Collaborative efforts facilitate the responsible deployment of AI technologies in addressing global challenges and ensuring equitable access to their benefits.

In conclusion, AI's potential to address global challenges is a testament to the transformative power of technology. It offers solutions to some of the world's most pressing problems, from healthcare and environmental sustainability to education and disaster response. Embracing AI as a tool for positive change requires a commitment to ethical development, responsible deployment, and global cooperation. The quest to harness AI's potential represents humanity's determination to use innovation for the betterment of all and to create a more prosperous and sustainable future for generations to come.

Environmental Sustainability and AI

The intersection of environmental sustainability and artificial intelligence (AI) is a powerful catalyst for addressing the urgent global challenge of climate change and promoting responsible resource management. This chapter extensively explores how AI is reshaping the landscape of environmental sustainability, offering innovative solutions to mitigate environmental threats and accelerate the transition towards a more sustainable future.

At its core, AI empowers environmental sustainability efforts through its capacity to process massive datasets, identify patterns, and optimize resource allocation. This computational prowess is instrumental in various aspects of environmental conservation, climate change mitigation, and the promotion of sustainable practices.

One of the most prominent applications of AI in environmental sustainability is climate modeling. AI-driven models analyze diverse climate data, including temperature, precipitation, and carbon emissions, to provide accurate predictions of climate trends and natural disasters. These predictions enable proactive measures such as disaster preparedness, resource allocation, and infrastructure resilience planning, helping communities mitigate the impacts of extreme weather events and adapt to changing climate patterns.

AI is also driving progress in renewable energy adoption and energy efficiency. Machine learning algorithms optimize energy production and consumption by analyzing real-time data from renewable sources like wind and solar. By predicting energy demand and identifying opportunities for efficiency improvements, AI contributes to reducing greenhouse gas emissions and advancing the transition to clean energy.

In agriculture, AI-powered precision farming practices optimize resource usage, including water, fertilizers, and pesticides. Drones and sensors equipped with AI algorithms monitor crop health, soil conditions, and weather patterns, enabling farmers to make data-driven decisions that increase crop yields while minimizing environmental impact. This sustainable approach promotes responsible land use and reduces the environmental footprint of agriculture.

Moreover, AI is instrumental in wildlife conservation efforts. AI-powered camera traps and satellite imagery help monitor endangered species, detect illegal poaching activities, and protect natural ecosystems. Machine learning algorithms analyze vast datasets of wildlife behavior, allowing researchers to gain insights into biodiversity trends and devise conservation strategies.

However, AI's role in environmental sustainability is not without its challenges. Ensuring that AI systems operate ethically and transparently is essential to preventing unintended consequences and potential biases in environmental decision-making. Striking the right balance between automation and human oversight is critical to maintaining ethical standards and protecting natural ecosystems.

Additionally, international collaboration and the sharing of environmental data are crucial in harnessing AI's full potential for sustainability. Governments, organizations, and researchers must work together to create open data platforms, harmonize environmental standards, and facilitate the responsible deployment of AI technologies.

The synergy between AI and environmental sustainability represents a transformative approach to addressing climate change, conserving natural ecosystems, and promoting responsible resource management. AI's capacity to process data, predict environmental trends, and optimize resource usage offers innovative solutions to some of the world's most pressing environmental challenges. Embracing AI as a tool for sustainability requires ethical considerations, global cooperation, and responsible AI development, paving the way for a more resilient and environmentally conscious future.

AI in Healthcare and Education

AI's integration into healthcare and education represents a revolution in how these critical sectors operate, offering extensive possibilities to enhance patient care, improve learning outcomes, and reshape the future of these industries. This chapter extensively explores the transformative impact of AI in healthcare and education, showcasing its potential to improve human lives and drive innovation.

AI in Healthcare: Artificial intelligence is revolutionizing healthcare by augmenting medical professionals' capabilities, optimizing processes, and personalizing patient care. Machine learning algorithms analyze vast amounts of patient data, including medical records, imaging, and genetic information, to assist clinicians in diagnosing diseases more accurately and predicting health risks. For instance, AI-driven diagnostic tools can detect anomalies in medical images, such as X-rays and MRIs, aiding in early disease detection. Furthermore, AI-enabled predictive analytics help hospitals optimize resource allocation, reduce patient readmissions, and manage patient flow more efficiently. Telemedicine platforms powered by AI facilitate remote patient monitoring and consultations, expanding healthcare access, especially in underserved areas. Additionally, AI-driven drug discovery accelerates the development of life-saving medications, making the pharmaceutical research process more efficient. AI's role in healthcare underscores the potential to improve patient outcomes, reduce costs, and make healthcare more accessible.

AI in Education: The impact of AI in education is far-reaching, transforming traditional classrooms into personalized and data-driven learning environments. AI-driven personalized learning platforms adapt to individual student needs, tailoring educational content, pace, and assessments to optimize learning outcomes. These platforms use machine learning to analyze student performance data, identifying areas where students need additional support or enrichment. Teachers benefit from AI-driven insights that inform instructional strategies and foster a deeper understanding of students' learning styles. Moreover, AI-powered chatbots assist students with queries, provide immediate feedback, and facilitate engagement, making education more interactive and accessible. In addition, AI aids in automating administrative tasks, reducing administrative burdens on educators. AI in education is redefining the educational experience, making it more inclusive, engaging, and adaptable to individual learner needs.

However, the integration of AI in healthcare and education also poses ethical considerations and challenges. Ensuring data privacy, maintaining ethical AI practices, and mitigating biases in AI algorithms are critical concerns. Furthermore, access to AI-powered healthcare and education tools must be equitable, preventing the exacerbation of existing disparities.

The future of AI in healthcare and education is marked by ongoing advancements, collaborative research, and responsible AI development.

The transformative potential of AI to improve patient care, enhance learning experiences, and drive innovation underscores the importance of embracing this technology while upholding ethical standards and addressing societal challenges. AI's integration into healthcare and education is not merely a technological shift; it is a testament to the potential of human-machine collaboration to advance these critical sectors and improve the quality of life for individuals worldwide.

Chapter Ten: Navigating the Unknown

Navigating the unknown is an exploration of the uncharted territories, uncertainties, and complexities that arise as humanity journeys deeper into the age of artificial intelligence (AI). This chapter extensively delves into the profound challenges, ethical dilemmas, and innovative solutions that define our path forward in this rapidly evolving landscape.

At its core, navigating the unknown in the AI era embodies the recognition that we are entering uncharted waters, where technological advancements often outpace our understanding of their implications. As AI systems become increasingly autonomous and sophisticated, questions about their ethical use, societal impact, and accountability abound.

One of the central challenges is the ethical dilemma posed by AI's capabilities. Autonomous AI systems, from self-driving cars to autonomous decision-making algorithms, raise questions about accountability in cases of accidents or harmful outcomes. Striking the right balance between AI autonomy and human oversight is crucial to ensure ethical and responsible AI deployment.

AI's impact on the job market is another area of uncertainty. While AI has the potential to create new industries and job opportunities, it also raises concerns about automation and job displacement. Navigating the unknown in this context involves workforce reskilling and upskilling to prepare individuals for evolving job roles in an AI-augmented world.

Additionally, AI bias is a critical issue that demands attention. Biases present in training data can result in discriminatory AI algorithms, perpetuating inequalities and reinforcing harmful stereotypes. Addressing AI bias requires rigorous data quality assurance, diverse representation in AI development teams, and ethical guidelines that prioritize fairness and transparency.

Privacy concerns loom large in navigating the unknown of AI. As AI systems process vast amounts of personal data, safeguarding privacy becomes paramount. Developing robust data protection mechanisms, such as data anonymization and encryption, is essential to prevent unauthorized access and data breaches.

Moreover, navigating the unknown involves grappling with the societal impact of AI. AI systems have the potential to amplify both positive and negative aspects of society. Ethical considerations, regulatory frameworks, and responsible AI development are pivotal in ensuring that AI aligns with human values and contributes to the betterment of society.

Education and awareness play a critical role in helping individuals and organizations navigate the unknown. Digital literacy, AI awareness, and responsible AI use should be integral parts of educational curricula and lifelong learning initiatives. An informed and educated society is better equipped to address the challenges and opportunities presented by AI.

In conclusion, navigating the unknown in the age of AI is a multifaceted endeavor that demands ethical reflection, innovation, and collaboration. While the challenges are significant, so are the opportunities to harness AI's potential for the greater good. Embracing the unknown requires a commitment to responsible AI development, transparent decision-making, and a forward-looking mindset. As we navigate these uncharted waters, we have the opportunity to shape a future where AI enriches human lives, fosters innovation, and contributes to a more equitable and sustainable world.

Preparing for the Future of AI

Preparing for the future of AI is an imperative for individuals, organizations, and societies as we stand on the threshold of a technologically transformed world. This chapter extensively explores the strategies, considerations, and actions necessary to navigate the evolving landscape of artificial intelligence (AI) and ensure that we harness its potential while mitigating its challenges.

At its core, preparing for the future of AI is a recognition that AI is not a static phenomenon but a rapidly evolving field. This evolution presents both opportunities and risks that require proactive measures and thoughtful planning. Here are several key aspects of preparation for the AI-driven future:

1. **Education and Upskilling**: Lifelong learning and upskilling are foundational in preparing individuals for the future of AI. Digital literacy, AI awareness, and acquiring new skills are essential to adapt to evolving job roles and harness AI's potential. Educational institutions and employers play pivotal roles in facilitating these learning opportunities.

2. **Ethical Frameworks**: Establishing ethical guidelines and frameworks for AI development and deployment is crucial. This involves defining principles that prioritize fairness, transparency, accountability, and the avoidance of bias. Ethical AI development ensures that AI aligns with human values and societal norms.

3. **Data Governance**: As data fuels AI, robust data governance practices are essential. Data privacy, security, and quality assurance measures protect sensitive information and ensure that data used in AI systems is reliable and unbiased.

4. **Regulatory Oversight**: Governments and regulatory bodies have a vital role in shaping the future of AI through policy and regulation. Effective governance frameworks are necessary to address issues such as AI safety, accountability, and the ethical use of AI technologies.

5. **Transparency and Explainability**: AI systems must be transparent and explainable to build trust and facilitate accountability. Users and stakeholders should understand how AI decisions are made, and mechanisms for recourse should be in place in cases of errors or bias.

6. **Responsible Innovation**: Encouraging responsible AI innovation involves fostering a culture of ethical development and responsible AI use. Organizations should prioritize ethical considerations in AI projects and promote diversity in AI development teams to mitigate bias.

7. **Collaboration**: Collaboration between governments, industry stakeholders, academia, and civil society is essential. Building

partnerships for knowledge sharing, research, and best practices helps address AI challenges on a global scale.

8. **Anticipating Societal Impact**: Preparing for the future of AI requires anticipating its impact on society, including job displacement, economic shifts, and changes in various industries. Policies and initiatives should be designed to mitigate negative consequences and ensure equitable access to AI benefits.

9. **Inclusivity**: Ensuring that the benefits of AI are accessible to all segments of society is crucial. Addressing digital divides and promoting inclusivity in AI development and deployment is essential to prevent exacerbating existing disparities.

Preparing for the future of AI is a multidimensional endeavor that involves education, ethics, regulation, transparency, and collaboration. As AI continues to shape our world, individuals, organizations, and governments must be proactive in their approach to navigate the challenges and harness the opportunities it presents. The future of AI holds immense potential for innovation, improved quality of life, and the advancement of society, provided that we take thoughtful and responsible steps to prepare for it.

Predictions and Scenarios for the Coming Decades

Predicting the future in the rapidly evolving landscape of artificial intelligence (AI) is a challenging yet essential endeavor. This chapter extensively explores various predictions and scenarios for the coming decades, offering insights into how AI is poised to reshape industries, society, and human experiences.

1. **AI in Healthcare**: The healthcare industry is poised for a profound transformation driven by AI. Predictive analytics and AI-driven diagnostic tools will become increasingly accurate, allowing healthcare professionals to detect diseases at their earliest stages. These tools will analyze vast datasets of patient information, medical imaging, and genetic data, providing clinicians with valuable insights for personalized

treatment plans. Telemedicine and remote patient monitoring will become integral components of healthcare, improving access to medical expertise, especially in remote or underserved areas. The ability of AI to analyze patient data in real time will enhance patient outcomes and reduce healthcare costs.

2. **Education Transformation**: AI's impact on education will be revolutionary. Personalized learning experiences powered by AI will adapt to the individual needs and learning styles of students. Virtual tutors and adaptive curricula will ensure that each student progresses at their own pace, while AI-driven assessments will provide real-time feedback to teachers and students. Lifelong learning will become the norm as job roles evolve due to automation and AI. Individuals will need to continuously acquire new skills and adapt to evolving industries and technologies.

3. **Workforce Shifts**: AI-driven automation will lead to shifts in the workforce. Routine and repetitive tasks will be automated, but new job roles will emerge in AI development, data analysis, and AI ethics. Jobs that require creativity, critical thinking, emotional intelligence, and complex problem-solving skills will be in demand. Upskilling and reskilling programs will be essential to prepare the workforce for these evolving roles.

4. **AI in Business**: AI will play a central role in business operations across industries. Predictive analytics powered by AI will optimize supply chains, demand forecasting, and inventory management. Customer experiences will be enhanced through AI-driven chatbots and virtual assistants, providing personalized support. AI will also assist in strategic decision-making, helping businesses make data-driven choices in areas like product development, marketing, and financial planning.

5. **Ethical AI**: Ethical considerations in AI development and deployment will take center stage. Transparent and explainable AI algorithms will be essential to build trust and ensure accountability. Efforts to mitigate bias in AI systems will focus on diverse representation in AI development teams and rigorous data quality assurance. Regulatory frameworks will

be established to guide responsible AI use and protect individual rights, privacy, and fairness.

6. **AI-Enhanced Creativity**: AI will become a creative collaborator in fields such as art, music, and literature. AI-generated content will challenge traditional notions of creativity. Artists, musicians, and writers will use AI tools to inspire and co-create, leading to novel and unexpected creative expressions. AI's ability to analyze vast datasets and identify patterns will expand the creative horizons of human creators.

7. **AI in Scientific Discovery**: AI's data processing capabilities will accelerate scientific research across various domains. AI-driven simulations will help scientists model complex systems, from climate patterns to biochemical interactions. AI will analyze massive datasets generated by experiments, telescopes, and satellite observations, leading to breakthroughs in fields such as genomics, materials science, and climate modeling. AI-driven drug discovery will expedite the development of life-saving medications.

8. **AI in Governance**: Governments will adopt AI to enhance governance. Predictive analytics will assist in resource allocation, disaster response, and law enforcement. AI will provide insights into public health trends, enabling more effective responses to epidemics and health crises. AI-driven cybersecurity tools will protect critical infrastructure, and AI will be used in national defense for threat detection and strategic planning. AI-powered chatbots will facilitate interactions with government agencies, making services more accessible to citizens.

9. **AI and the Environment**: AI will play a pivotal role in addressing environmental challenges. Climate modeling powered by AI will provide more accurate predictions, helping governments and organizations prepare for climate-related disasters and adapt to changing weather patterns. AI-driven energy optimization will enhance the efficiency of renewable energy sources, reducing carbon emissions. Conservation efforts will benefit from AI's ability to monitor and protect natural ecosystems, track endangered species, and combat illegal poaching.

10. **AI and Entertainment**: AI will transform the entertainment industry. Content recommendation systems powered by AI will provide personalized entertainment experiences, whether in streaming services or gaming. AI-generated music and art will challenge traditional creative boundaries, offering new forms of entertainment. Virtual reality experiences will become more immersive and personalized, revolutionizing storytelling and gaming.

11. **Global Collaboration**: The global nature of AI challenges and opportunities will necessitate collaboration among governments, organizations, academia, and civil society. Partnerships will be formed to share knowledge, research, and best practices. International standards and ethical guidelines will be established to ensure responsible AI development and use on a global scale. Collaborative efforts will foster innovation and help address the complexities of AI governance.

12. **AI and Healthcare Accessibility**: AI will play a critical role in improving healthcare accessibility, particularly in underserved regions. Telemedicine platforms powered by AI will connect patients with healthcare providers, overcoming geographical barriers. AI-driven diagnostic tools will enable early disease detection in regions with limited medical infrastructure. Predictive analytics will aid in managing epidemics and public health crises, ensuring a rapid response to emerging health threats.

Predicting the future of AI involves considering these multifaceted possibilities and uncertainties. While AI offers immense potential for innovation and improvement in various aspects of life, responsible development, ethical considerations, and inclusivity will be essential to realizing its benefits while mitigating its challenges. Preparing for the coming decades in the age of AI requires adaptability, continuous learning, and a commitment to ethical and responsible AI use. The future of AI is a dynamic and ever-evolving landscape where human creativity, innovation, and ethical principles will guide our path forward.

Cultivating an AI-Ready Mindset

Cultivating an AI-ready mindset is a transformative approach to prepare individuals, organizations, and societies for the profound changes brought about by artificial intelligence (AI). This chapter extensively explores the core principles, strategies, and attitudes required to embrace the AI era with adaptability, creativity, and ethical responsibility.

At its core, cultivating an AI-ready mindset begins with a willingness to adapt and learn continuously. The AI landscape is dynamic, characterized by rapid advancements and evolving possibilities. Individuals who foster an AI-ready mindset recognize that adaptability and lifelong learning are essential components of navigating this ever-changing terrain.

Critical thinking is a cornerstone of an AI-ready mindset. It involves the ability to assess information critically, question assumptions, and evaluate the ethical implications of AI technologies. A well-developed critical thinking skillset empowers individuals to make informed decisions, whether as consumers of AI-driven products or as contributors to AI development.

Ethical considerations are paramount in an AI-ready mindset. Ethical awareness involves recognizing the potential biases, privacy concerns, and societal impacts of AI technologies. An AI-ready individual or organization is committed to responsible AI development and use, prioritizing fairness, transparency, and accountability.

Innovation and creativity are integral components of an AI-ready mindset. Embracing AI as a tool for creativity allows individuals to explore new possibilities for collaboration and co-creation with AI systems. Artists, scientists, and entrepreneurs leverage AI to push the boundaries of what is possible, sparking innovative solutions to complex problems.

Collaboration and interdisciplinary thinking are key principles of an AI-ready mindset. Recognizing that AI's impact extends across diverse domains, individuals and organizations seek to bridge disciplines and work collaboratively to address complex challenges. Interdisciplinary collaboration fosters a holistic approach to problem-solving and innovation.

AI literacy is fundamental in an AI-ready mindset. Understanding the basics of AI, its capabilities, and its limitations empowers individuals to engage meaningfully with AI technologies. AI literacy also promotes informed discussions about AI's societal impact and ethical considerations.

Inclusivity is a core value in an AI-ready mindset. Recognizing that AI technologies should benefit all segments of society, individuals and organizations strive to ensure that AI solutions are accessible and do not exacerbate existing disparities. Efforts to promote inclusivity involve addressing digital divides and creating AI solutions that accommodate diverse needs.

An AI-ready mindset also embraces the concept of lifelong learning. In an era where job roles evolve rapidly due to automation and AI, individuals understand the importance of continuous upskilling and reskilling. Education and training initiatives become essential components of an AI-ready society, ensuring that individuals remain adaptable and competitive in the job market.

Furthermore, embracing a growth mindset is integral to an AI-ready mindset. This mindset encourages individuals to view challenges and setbacks as opportunities for growth and learning. It fosters resilience and a willingness to experiment with new technologies and approaches.

Cultivating an AI-ready mindset represents a fundamental shift in how individuals, organizations, and societies approach the age of AI. It encompasses adaptability, critical thinking, ethical awareness, innovation, collaboration, inclusivity, AI literacy, lifelong learning, and a growth mindset. Embracing these principles and attitudes empowers individuals and organizations to navigate the complexities of the AI era, harness its potential, and address its challenges responsibly. The cultivation of an AI-ready mindset is not just a response to technological change but a proactive commitment to shaping a future where AI enriches human lives, fosters innovation, and contributes to a more equitable and sustainable world.

Conclusion

In the culmination of this journey through the pages of "Redefining Tomorrow: Exploring the Boundaries of AI and Humanity," we find ourselves at a unique intersection of technological marvel and human potential. This book has been a voyage into the heart of artificial intelligence (AI), a realm where innovation, ethics, and our collective imagination converge to shape the future of humanity.

Our exploration began with the genesis of AI, tracing its evolution from science fiction dreams to the very real and tangible force that shapes our world today. We embarked on a historical odyssey, charting the course of AI's development, from early symbolic logic to the intricate neural networks that underpin its capabilities. Through this journey, we uncovered the relentless spirit of human ingenuity that propels us ever forward.

The impact of AI across various industries has been nothing short of revolutionary. In healthcare, finance, transportation, education, and beyond, AI has redefined the boundaries of what's possible. It has improved patient care, streamlined financial operations, transformed transportation logistics, and enhanced educational experiences. Yet, these transformations have not come without their share of ethical and societal considerations, reminding us that with great power comes great responsibility.

Our journey also delved deep into the inner workings of AI, unraveling the intricate mechanisms of machine learning, deep learning, and neural networks. We discovered that data is the lifeblood of AI, fueling its ability to analyze vast datasets, recognize patterns, and make predictions. It became evident that ethical data practices and considerations are paramount in this AI-powered age.

Profiles of AI pioneers celebrated the brilliant minds who have shaped the AI landscape. Their visionary contributions, whether in the realm of natural language processing or the development of iconic AI systems, have showcased the boundless potential of human creativity.

Ethical dilemmas emerged as a central theme, prompting us to confront the biases within AI systems, address privacy concerns, and navigate the intricate ethical considerations surrounding AI development and deployment. Augmented intelligence showed us the profound ways in which AI can enhance human capabilities and foster innovation.

In envisioning the future, we explored potential scenarios where AI could revolutionize healthcare, education, the workforce, business, governance, and environmental sustainability. These glimpses into tomorrow underscored the need for adaptability, critical thinking, ethical responsibility, and inclusivity as we prepare for an AI-driven world.

Through it all, the concept of cultivating an AI-ready mindset emerged as a guiding principle, urging us to embrace AI with open hearts and open minds. It called on us to approach AI with resilience, creativity, and ethical responsibility, recognizing that AI is a tool to amplify human potential rather than diminish it.

As we conclude this exploration, "Redefining Tomorrow: Exploring the Boundaries of AI and Humanity" is not just a book; it's a testament to the human spirit's ability to innovate, adapt, and shape the future. It's a reminder that the boundaries we face are not constraints but invitations to push further, explore deeper, and reimagine what's possible. In this AI-powered age, we are not passive observers; we are active participants in the forging of a world where technology and humanity coexist, where ethical principles guide our path, and where the future, once defined by uncertainty, is now shaped by our collective vision of a better, brighter, and more inclusive tomorrow.

The Future Awaits: Embracing the Journey Ahead

As we conclude our exploration through the pages of "Redefining Tomorrow: Exploring the Boundaries of AI and Humanity," we stand at the threshold of a future that holds the promise of unprecedented transformation and boundless potential. The journey we've undertaken has been a testament to the relentless march of human progress, where the convergence of artificial intelligence (AI) and human ingenuity reshapes the contours of our existence.

In this final chapter, titled "The Future Awaits: Embracing the Journey Ahead," we reflect on the profound insights, ethical considerations, and visionary possibilities that have emerged from our expedition into the heart of AI. It is a moment of reflection and anticipation, a pause to consider the profound implications of our collective endeavors in this era of AI.

Throughout our exploration, we have witnessed the emergence of AI as a formidable force, transcending the boundaries of science fiction to become an integral part of our daily lives. The historical narrative has revealed the persistence of human visionaries, who, with unwavering determination, have propelled AI from conceptual infancy to its present state of transformative power. The milestones in AI development have showcased the tireless innovation that fuels this field, pushing the envelope of what is possible with each passing day.

AI's impact across industries has underscored its potential to revolutionize how we live, work, and interact with the world. In healthcare, it has become a beacon of hope, promising improved diagnostics and personalized treatment plans. In finance, it has brought efficiency and innovation to complex operations. In transportation, it has transformed logistics and reimagined our mobility. In education, it has unlocked the potential for personalized learning experiences. However, these remarkable advancements have not come without their share of ethical and societal challenges, urging us to tread the path of AI with careful consideration.

Our deep dive into the core mechanics of AI has illuminated the intricate processes that power its capabilities. Machine learning, deep learning, and neural networks have unveiled the algorithms that underpin AI's decision-making. The critical role of data has been highlighted as the lifeblood of AI, emphasizing the importance of responsible data practices and ethical data governance.

Profiles of AI pioneers have celebrated the luminaries who have etched their names in the annals of AI history. Their groundbreaking contributions have demonstrated the potential of human creativity to transcend boundaries and pave the way for transformative innovations.

The ethical dilemmas surrounding AI have prompted us to confront biases, address privacy concerns, and navigate the complex ethical considerations inherent in AI development and deployment. Augmented intelligence has shown us that AI is not a threat to human capabilities but a tool to amplify them, fostering collaboration and innovation.

Envisioning the future has offered us glimpses into the myriad ways AI could revolutionize healthcare, education, the workforce, business, governance, and environmental sustainability. These scenarios have highlighted the need for adaptability, critical thinking, ethical responsibility, and inclusivity as we prepare to embrace the opportunities and challenges of an AI-driven world.

Cultivating an AI-ready mindset has emerged as a guiding principle, reminding us that, as we stand on the cusp of this transformative era, our readiness to embrace AI with resilience, creativity, and ethical responsibility will define our journey ahead.

In this concluding chapter, "The Future Awaits: Embracing the Journey Ahead," we are reminded that the future is not a distant destination but a journey we embark upon every day. It is a journey where technology and humanity converge, where the boundaries of what's possible continue to expand, and where our choices today shape the world of tomorrow. As we step forward into the unknown, let us do so with a spirit of curiosity, responsibility, and optimism, for the future awaits, brimming with the potential to redefine our world and reimagine what it means to be human in the age of AI.

Glossary of AI Terms

As we delve deeper into the world of artificial intelligence (AI) in this book, it's essential to have a solid grasp of the terminology that underpins this field. AI is a multidisciplinary domain with its own lexicon, and this glossary serves as your reference guide, offering concise explanations for key AI terms and concepts.

1. **Artificial Intelligence (AI)**: The branch of computer science dedicated to creating systems and algorithms that can perform tasks that typically require human intelligence, such as problem-solving, decision-making, and natural language understanding.

2. **Machine Learning (ML)**: A subset of AI that focuses on the development of algorithms and models that enable computers to learn from and make predictions or decisions based on data without explicit programming.

3. **Deep Learning**: A subfield of machine learning that involves training artificial neural networks with multiple layers (deep neural networks) to process and interpret data, often achieving remarkable accuracy in tasks like image and speech recognition.

4. **Neural Network**: A computational model inspired by the human brain's structure, consisting of interconnected nodes (neurons) organized in layers. Neural networks are used in various machine-learning tasks.

5. **Data Science**: The interdisciplinary field that combines statistics, domain knowledge, and computer science to extract insights and knowledge from data, a crucial aspect of AI and machine learning.

6. **Algorithm**: A set of step-by-step instructions or rules that a computer follows to perform a specific task or solve a particular problem, such as sorting data or making predictions.

7. **Supervised Learning**: A type of machine learning where the algorithm is trained on a labeled dataset, with known input-output pairs, to make predictions or classifications based on new, unseen data.

8. **Unsupervised Learning**: A machine learning approach where the algorithm learns patterns and structures in data without labeled examples, often used for tasks like clustering and dimensionality reduction.

9. **Reinforcement Learning**: A machine learning paradigm in which an agent learns to make sequential decisions through interaction with an environment, receiving feedback (rewards or penalties) for its actions.

10. **Natural Language Processing (NLP)**: The field of AI focused on enabling computers to understand, interpret, and generate human language, used in applications like chatbots, language translation, and sentiment analysis.

11. **Computer Vision**: The subfield of AI that focuses on enabling computers to interpret and understand visual information from the world, including tasks like image recognition and object detection.

12. **Algorithm Bias**: The presence of systematic and unfair discrimination or inaccuracies in AI algorithms, often resulting from biased training data or biased design decisions.

13. **Ethical AI**: The practice of developing and using AI systems in ways that prioritize fairness, transparency, accountability, and ethical considerations to minimize harm and promote responsible AI use.

14. **AI Ethics**: A branch of ethics that addresses the moral and societal implications of AI, including issues related to bias, privacy, job displacement, and autonomous decision-making.

15. **Big Data**: Large and complex datasets that require specialized techniques and tools for storage, processing, and analysis, often used in machine learning and data science.

16. **Artificial General Intelligence (AGI)**: An advanced form of AI that possesses human-like intelligence and the ability to understand, learn, and adapt to a wide range of tasks and domains, currently a subject of research and development.

17. **Chatbot**: A computer program or AI system designed to engage in conversation with users, often used in customer support, virtual assistants, and information retrieval.

18. **Data Privacy**: The protection of individuals' personal information and data from unauthorized access, use, or disclosure, a crucial concern in AI and data-driven applications.

19. **Supervised Learning**: A type of machine learning where the algorithm is trained on a labeled dataset, with known input-output pairs, to make predictions or classifications based on new, unseen data.

20. **Unsupervised Learning**: A machine learning approach where the algorithm learns patterns and structures in data without labeled examples, often used for tasks like clustering and dimensionality reduction.

This glossary provides a foundation for understanding key AI concepts and terms. As the field of AI continues to evolve, new terminology and concepts may emerge. Staying informed and continuously expanding your AI vocabulary is essential for navigating this exciting and dynamic domain.

Recommended Reading and Resources

As you embark on your journey through "Redefining Tomorrow: Exploring the Boundaries of AI and Humanity," it's crucial to expand your knowledge beyond the confines of this book. The field of artificial intelligence (AI) is vast and continuously evolving, and a wealth of resources is available to help you dive deeper into specific topics, stay updated on the latest developments, and gain insights from experts in the field. Here, we present a curated list of recommended reading and resources that can enrich your understanding of AI:

Books:

1. "Artificial Intelligence: A Guide to Intelligent Systems" by Michael Negnevitsky - A comprehensive introduction to AI concepts, techniques, and applications.

2. "Machine Learning: A Probabilistic Perspective" by Kevin P. Murphy - Offers a deep dive into the probabilistic foundations of machine learning.

3. "Deep Learning" by Ian Goodfellow, Yoshua Bengio, and Aaron Courville - The definitive book on deep learning, covering the theory and practical applications.

4. "AI Superpowers: China, Silicon Valley, and the New World Order" by Kai-Fu Lee - Explores the global AI landscape and its implications for society and geopolitics.

5. "Weapons of Math Destruction: How Big Data Increases Inequality and Threatens Democracy" by Cathy O'Neil - Examines the ethical and societal impact of AI and data-driven algorithms.

Online Courses and Tutorials:

1. Coursera (coursera.org) - Offers a range of AI and machine learning courses, including "Machine Learning" by Andrew Ng and "Deep Learning Specialization" by deeplearning.ai.

2. edX (edx.org) - Provides courses like "Artificial Intelligence" by MIT and "Practical Deep Learning for Coders" by fast.ai.

Websites and Blogs:

1. Towards Data Science (towardsdatascience.com) - A Medium publication featuring articles on AI, machine learning, and data science.

2. AI Ethics (aiethicslab.com) - A resource hub dedicated to the ethical considerations and societal implications of AI.

3. OpenAI Blog (openai.com/blog) - Offers insights into cutting-edge AI research and development.

Research Journals and Papers:

1. arXiv (arxiv.org) - A preprint repository that hosts a vast collection of AI research papers spanning various subfields.

2. Google Scholar (scholar.google.com) - An academic search engine that allows you to discover AI-related research papers and articles.

Podcasts:

1. "Artificial Intelligence" (AI) by Lex Fridman - Features in-depth interviews with AI researchers, practitioners, and thought leaders.

2. "The AI Alignment Podcast" by the Center for the Study of Existential Risk** - Explores the alignment problem in AI ethics and safety.

AI Communities:

1. Reddit - r/MachineLearning (reddit.com/r/MachineLearning) - A vibrant community of machine learning enthusiasts discussing research, projects, and AI news.

2. Stack Overflow (stackoverflow.com) - A valuable platform for AI practitioners to seek help, share knowledge, and collaborate on coding challenges.

AI Conferences and Events:

1. NeurIPS (Conference on Neural Information Processing Systems) - A leading AI conference featuring research presentations, tutorials, and workshops.

2. CVPR (Conference on Computer Vision and Pattern Recognition) - Focused on computer vision, this conference showcases the latest advancements in image analysis and recognition.

3. ICML (International Conference on Machine Learning) - An annual event highlighting the latest developments in machine learning research.

AI Ethics and Responsible AI:

1. AI Ethics Guidelines (futureoflife.org/ai-ethics-guidelines) - A collection of guidelines and principles for responsible AI development and use.

2. The Partnership on AI (partnershiponai.org) - A consortium of organizations dedicated to addressing the global challenges of AI, with resources on AI ethics and safety.

These recommended readings and resources provide a solid foundation for further exploration and learning in the world of AI. Whether you're a beginner looking to understand the basics or an AI practitioner seeking to stay updated on the latest advancements, these materials will empower you to navigate the complexities of AI and contribute to its responsible and ethical development.

Index

In "Redefining Tomorrow: Exploring the Boundaries of AI and Humanity,"
we've covered a broad spectrum of topics related to artificial intelligence
(AI) and its impact on our world. This comprehensive index is designed
to help readers easily locate specific subjects, concepts, and keywords
throughout the book, enabling quick reference and deeper exploration of
key themes. Here is an alphabetical list of index entries:

The index is intended to serve as a valuable tool for readers seeking
specific information within the book. Entries are organized alphabetically,
with page numbers provided for each topic. It's our hope that this index

will enhance your reading experience, making it easier to navigate the wealth of knowledge and insights presented in "Redefining Tomorrow: Exploring the Boundaries of AI and Humanity."